IRIDESCENCE

An Invitation to Awaken to the Light of Being

MICAELA FOX

"In your light do we see light."

Psalm 36:9

Dedicated to my grandma,
one who always saw the prism of light in me.

ir·i·des·cence | \ ˌir-ə-ˈde-sᵊn(t)s \

Definition of *iridescence*

I: a lustrous rainbow-like play of color caused by differential refraction of light waves (as from a prism or soap bubble) that tends to change as the angle of view changes: "*Many colors found in nature are produced by pigmentation, which simply absorbs certain wavelengths of light and reflects others. Iridescence, however, occurs when an object's physical structure causes light waves to combine with one another, a phenomenon known as interference. In constructive interference, light waves combine so that the crests and troughs line up to reinforce each other, increasing the vibrancy of the reflected color. Destructive interference occurs when the crests and troughs cancel each other out to dim the color. Thus, as the observer's viewing angle shifts, the colors of the iridescent object change depending on the varying degrees of constructive and destructive interference.*"

—*Yale Scientific*

While traveling through Europe, then picking up her life and moving from the coast of California to Texas, Micaela explores the depths of divine beauty, unceasing joy, heartbreak, anxiety, grief, the wildness of femininity, and the lavish gift of mystical union.

This is a journey through the full spectrum and glory of what it means to be human, where we find God in the everyday intertwining of our humanity and His divinity.

NOTE FROM THE AUTHOR

When I was seven years old, I vividly remember the moment I watched shafts of light bleed into my family's living room through our arched window. It was early morning, when everything felt still, innocent, and renewed. Peace I had never known washed over me like the light I was watching flow into my living room. My breath grew deeper, my lungs expanding as rest filled every part of me like a gentle ocean breeze. I couldn't stop gazing at the light in wonder, studying it and the dance of tiny, floating particles that I would have never noticed without its illumination. Joy bubbled in me as I observed the light rest softly on the carpet and shimmer against the walls. I had to draw near. As I reached out to touch it, a rainbow appeared on my hand from the bending of the light through the window.

This book is dedicated to that moment. To childlike wonder. To noticing the allure of light in the everyday mundane, where we and our world are deeply filled with color. Like a soap bubble that you blew from a stick as a kid carries the rainbow in the light's refraction—that same iridescence is inside and all around us.

If only we would come awake, be present, and learn to draw near to the shafts of light within and around us.

My heart burns for you to be awakened to every reflection of light inside of yourself, in all your pieces, in all the mundanity. I long that you would be sober to the reality of God in everything and the depth of beauty that is present in you and in this life: this shimmering rainbow of light that can be seen differently at every angle, in every facet of emotion, grief, joy, anxiety, confusion, monotony, heartbreak, or overwhelming love.

The Light is never *not* present; it is waiting to be discovered and known in everything.

In this life, we too often try to rid ourselves of our humanity out of fear—fear of rejection, abandonment, disconnection. We try to avoid those things we're afraid of, the fractures of our being, the frustration of longing for the "more" we deeply know we were made for, all the things we cannot control.

We fight against our humanity; yet being restored to what it truly means to be human is the entire point of this existence. We are on the pilgrimage of being reconciled back to our origin: union with a God who is very alive and with us, and the truth that we are very good and loved *in the midst of it all.*

My prayer in writing this is that any shame of the human experience would be completely uprooted, and you would be able to relate to and discover the face of God in every crevice of your being.

In every single angle there is light waiting for us to draw near and touch it.

I invite you to join me; let's make contact with the light and *become iridescent.*

With love,

Micaela Fox

micaelapfox.com

To discover further writing from Micaela Fox, as well as
photographs and other entrepreneurial projects, scan the QR code above.

CONTENTS

Europe
The Refraction

America & Back to Europe
The Reflection

I'm longing to be honest
more than i've ever been.   I want to take off every mask,
                             efface every little shadow within,
                             and breathe deep again.

But i know,
if it's honest,
no matter how painful,
i'll pay attention —
for that's where the light is

You are a prism,
Iridescent
Through which the beauty,
The giving of the light of life,
refracts.

"As kids were afraid of the dark,
as adults we're afraid of the light."
—Elyssa Smith

Beauty both shouts and whispers,
it begs to question what's asleep within —
as it should — as we should rage again.

Let There Be Light

July 27, 2023
Nadia and Ryan's House
London, UK
11:20 p.m.

I'm longing to be honest,
more than I've ever been.

I want to take off every mask,
efface every little shadow within,
and breathe deep again.

I'm held tonight,
in four walls of a dear friend.

In a warm cozy bed,
yet anxiety is in my chest.

–It always hits in waves like this.

But I know, if it's honest,
no matter how painful,
I'll pay attention–
for that's where the light is.

Anxiety is simply this,

a closed door of the heart.

So I'll open up and expose it all!

Where I fear the most,
where honesty calls.

I want to, I have to,
let all the light in.

So let there be light!
Search me and know me,
flood identity into chaos!

Birth new worlds into existence,
by the power of Your voice,
inside my aching heart tonight.

Oh to let and to let,
again and again,

with an unlocked chest and wide open hands.

Illuminating Love
A prayer

Presence of illuminating love,
awaken my spirit into the bridal realm,
where we are fully one,
alive inside ascension,
flowing on the wind of your wings,
my love, my Dove.

Spirit of the knowledge of Christ,
pierce my heart awake.

Do not let my mind re-stitch the curtain of separation that you tore,
the train of your robe *a bridal veil, where all things you restore.*

Help me to bleed for you,
letting love cost me,
fully surrendered,
like you—*lowly, lowly, lowly.*

Hover over the waters of the deep,
be Lord over the chaos within me.

Yeshua, take out all the planks from my eyes,
open up all the blinds.

Never let disillusionment cause my heart to wane,
keep me tender—all my walls lowered by your mercy,
all my days.

Helper, guard my heart with the gift of forgiveness,
for bitterness is always a blind and misdirected lead.

Forever wash me,
by the blood and water spilled out at your side,
where you never leave *mine*
—teach me this new way of living.

Continually reconcile all of me
back to Eden.

Unfold all inner Truth,
remind me over and over of the love you infused,
all for me to continually whisper back,
"*My love, all for you.*"

...

Spirit, we need you, to see you,
to know the full resonance of Truth.

The acquainted one,
the bloody one,
the Lion and the Lamb.

Open our eyes with provoking light like a flood,
that we could fully receive when we hear you say,

"You are worth the cost I paid for with blood."

Where Goodbyes Don't Exist

July 19th, 2022
Corvus Coffee and Co.
Denver, Colorado
11:15 a.m.

There are things that are so beautiful:
the encompassing eyes of someone you love,
someone who knows you better than you know yourself.

The taste of quality espresso;
lying on the couch with the windows open to the smell of rain;
memories that make you laugh right before you fall asleep;
sampling each piece in a box of chocolates;
the warmth and smell of freshly cleaned sheets.

Snuggling golden retrievers while they lick your face;
the feeling of eating oversized bowls of pasta
with loved ones, *together, always just to be together*,
around a table.

Curious smiles from strangers;
cheering on marathon runners in a buzzing crowd;
handwritten notes by the coffee pot;
wearing that pair of jeans that fit just right;
the twirl of a sundress in an open field;
the innocence of a child's eyes;

throwback tunes on an old burned CD;
sweet nostalgia that soothes anxiety.

The deft touch of another's hand,
while tears roll down your face,
whispering, "*I understand.*"

—all of us carrying such faithful resilience.

This unending sharing of humanity,

      that is held in every room.

Could it be that loneliness,
any feeling of separateness,
disillusioned dissonance,
only exists in the mind?

Could it be so simple,
to let go of the narrowing confines—

to feel the light invading?

This miraculous gift of existence,
gratitude so weighty,
in the monotony, *just waiting*
to slow us down,

to envelop our skin like shafts of light
beaming through old friendly pines,
when we stop to look around—*finally still*,
fully present inside our own living rooms.
The wonder of it all,
falling through our bedroom window,
developing like a path to follow,
eroding through all our walls,
every single waking morning,
faithful to open our eyes,
always so loyal
to guide us home.

Can you hear it?
Distinct laughter you can recognize from anywhere,
of those you've shared tears with,
irreplaceable friends
in a dimly lit room holding that smooth,
undiluted whiskey.

In this room, filled with people you will always love,
where you make eye contact and realize,
you are altogether known and seen.

This is where goodbyes don't exist,
these are things
that live on in you forever.

Like the Leaves

July 23, 2022
The Lake House
Lake Eufaula, Oklahoma
9:33 p.m.

Without the wind,
the trees wouldn't rustle,
the clouds wouldn't roll
—all would cease.

Would seasons still come and go?
Or would change and growth revert to
a sort of dreadful stagnancy?

There's a patter of rain,
tapping, shimmering,
dancing on the tin roof above me.

The wind brought it here,
such a joyful, soothing melody.

The trees never fear or resist,
letting the rain drench them entirely.

Wind, your conviction is kind as a hug
that pursues and consoles my living body.

When I fear your shifting,
may I keep the reverence for your sovereignty.

May I be like the leaves in the trees,
totally surrendered to your movements,

your movements, only.

At the Periphery

July 28, 2022
Nadia and Ryan's Backyard
London, UK
2:22 p.m.

To understand, to truly listen,
you must reach out of your own condition.

Lean in, lift your chin,
pay attention.

Trees rustle in the wind, flowers bloom,
the day breathes, as we do.

There is a voice in the reverberations of being,
God's voice, that can be found in everything.

His gentle voice,
that is always speaking.

Even in this pen,
that marks, that spills
onto this paper,
that came from the trees.

The same trees that sway
in the breath of the wind,
all is a circle,
we are held within.

You see, I thought a bee died today,
but he was only sleeping,
he is no longer where he was resting.

How odd we can confuse
one of the deepest postures of rest
with the cloak of death.

Such stillness whispers to me,
"Look further, linger in the unknown,
just a little longer."

If only I would have remained,
been willing to change,
malleable to my own paradigm,
courageous enough to scale
the tightrope edges of my own perspective,
like a fish rising out of water,
an iridescent reflection.
Maybe, just maybe,

breath, life itself,
would have been revealed to me.

I would have been met
with understanding,
there, only at the periphery.

Felicity

July 30, 2022
Gosausee, Austria
3:33 p.m.

Beauty both shouts and whispers,
it begs to question what's asleep within—
as it should—as we should rage against.

There's reason the rocks cry out,
quiet, do you hear their sound?
Do you hear how they echo
your cries as you lay in bed at night?
Its ricochet calling out
until you're found.

This longing,
this magnificent, icy sea-green water,
these awe-filled glaciers hidden
among looming mountaintops.

In the distance.

This distance
that brings us to our knees.

The earth is always singing
to the human soul;
this is intimacy.

Would we be brave enough
to step into the miraculous being
of our very existence—
like the mountains—
so terrifying, so true?

Strip all the fear from our bones,
let beauty swell courage in us
and lead us hand in hand, home.

After all, maybe it wasn't felicity
that we needed, but a reminder,
something to do with majesty,
the power within
to defy passivity.

Choose to risk,
deeply love,
respond,
overcome,
reach out our hands,
and draw scary close
to the excruciating questions,
co-existing,

where the curtain rolls back,
where we're vulnerable and naked—

in the cool of the day,
where we ultimately discover

Presence.

In our deepest humane
joy and pain.

And here we find beauty that is ethereal.
And here we find clarity is inevitable.
And here we find worth immovable.
And here we find love encompassing, palpable.

Wonder

August 1, 2022
Mame Coffee Shop
Zurich, Switzerland
2:19 p.m.

I am drinking
the breath of God.

I've found Him in this coffee cup!
Delight is overflowing!

He's smiling at me,
while the brilliant light of the sun
is spilling over the green branches of the trees,
swimming into eyes, all of these eyes,
on these thrill-seeking streets!
I am a kid again, flying on a swing!

Here I wonder
how, for as long as we live,
we ache to understand

—but why must it all make sense?

The Triteness of Being

August 1, 2022
Mame Coffee Shop
Zurich, Switzerland
2:33 p.m.

Oh, how we can be forgetfully
human!

The hardest questions of life
are the most interesting!

How God hides Himself
just so we would draw near.

So find Him!

Silence is never lack of presence.

A way which cannot be observed,
only felt, deep in your bones
—like everything true.

We don't see it,
but the roots of the trees
in these city streets
are connecting, underneath,

and I know now,
they are just wanting

        to touch each other.

Unconditional love reaching to wear down what thickens
around our hearts and minds.

Would we wake up and see
not one thing is separated,
with attentive, open eyes?

Could we let the roots of these trees instruct
just how much we are integrated,
entangled and wholly one?

In every moment,
never separated.

Could we remember?

How to stay awake and authentic
when our fractured pieces feel
more comfortable than being whole—
when our wounds make us numb and hidden,
when we compartmentalize the soul.

How can we close the gap of what stands
between us and our own self-imposed tunnel vision?

How can we let light spill into us,
in the triteness of being,
and stay soft, soft, soft,
that God would find us
soberly singing.

Here,
would God find us,
fully awake—
remembering.

Anne Frank

August 2, 2022
The Anne Frank Museum
Zug, Switzerland

Refrain from being unwilling to turn your heart inside out;
it may feel like it, but withholding it never protects it.

Close your eyes, breathe deep,
feel the kindness of nature, the warm rain
on your hands, never failing to kindly provide,
showing you a faithfulness that is yours to keep.

Look and see how all of creation is for you,
open yourself up to the recollection of innate truth.

Hope—it is not distant,
or something to externally reach;
it is within—the very air we breathe.

Discover the unending goodness of humanity.

Feel liberation drawing near.
Feel yourself maturing.

...

I saw this—
kids colored pictures,
while in concentration camps.
Suffocated by grief, they still colored.

Chills went up my legs.

                    This is a reality—

to grieve does not mean
to be without hope.

Why should you choose despair?
Anne Frank never did.

Honey

August 2, 2022
Zug, Switzerland
12:13 a.m.

Bees are everywhere here,
they remind me of you—
rare, pure gentle honey, spilled out.

I'm not sure you realize
just how much
all of the dissonance still stings;
tears soaked on my bed sheets.

In you, I saw the galaxy.

Out beyond ideas of wrongdoing and rightdoing
there is a field. I'll meet you there."

—Rumi

Tension
A remembered thought

September 15, 2020
Redding, California
12:55 a.m.

Right and wrong, black and white,
Jesus was nailed in the middle of a cross
—not one side.
All of Truth is held in tension,
where mystery becomes the revelation.

"Being true to who we are, means carrying our spirit
like a candle in the center of our darkness."
—Mark Nepo

Incarnate

August 2, 2022
Zurich HB train station, Switzerland
12:08 p.m.

We are not compartmentalized,
our spirit is not divided against our minds—
as we think it is.

Oh, yes, does the mind not give us hell?
But any divide is the illusion in and of itself.

Cracks in the crevice,
hidden, suppressed pieces,
shadows that only bounce off what's real.

Our heart, all that we live from

—aching to emerge from the depths,
gasping in air at the surface.

Underwater, all of our emotions,
our body fighting at the breaks in the waves.

While it's only in yielding to the tides of grief
that sweep us up onto shore's relief.

Come up, come up for air—
breathe in love.

All is an invitation to relate,
God became incarnate.

"I have often thought about how the soul and the spirit
are really one thing, like the sun and its rays."
—St. Teresa of Avila, *The Interior Castle*

To Be Married

August 2, 2022
Zurich HB train station, Switzerland
12:40 p.m.

What we have learned
is that we are broken—

to be done away with.

Gnosticism and shame have taught us this.

Though, isn't shame,
all that which says "this is black and this is white!"
controlling and dualistic.

Anything that speaks dualism is a liar.
Evil always works like this.

Always in absolutes,
with intent to divorce
what is already joined

and cannot be broken.
But only in the state of the mind.

We are not at war against our humanity.
It is not something to cure but accept.

For when we die, it doesn't cease—
only our self-hatred, our striving.

Imago Dei! Heaven is inside of us!

It's not just somewhere we go when we die,
it is here and now—
so inhale the stars,
step into love, and realize
we are not broken.
We are whole.
Unravel from all the lies.

All is interrelated through an invisible bond.
So bind your life to the truth of your soul,
especially the cuts, the bruises, the shadows!

There is to be no divorce,

in the life of the heart and mind,
in every emotion and move of our bodies,

in the life of faith and truth,
amidst the reality of doubt and anxiety,
amidst all feeling and bleeding,
in the anguish and the peace,
in the joy and the grief,
in the bitter and the sweet,
It is all,

to be married.

Jesus did not just save our spirits
but our whole being, *everything.*

We are in union;

His blood swimming within us—
we cannot separate even if we tried.

Distance is always an illusion of the mind.

We are married.

No shame, no fracture internally.

This is how we're meant to breathe,
no more striving,
resting deeply in the radical glory and full spectrum of being.

Immersion & Euphoria

August 3, 2022
Solanos, Italy
1:57 p.m.

All the water that filled my shoes back home
poured out into the Mediterranean Sea today.

Here I am weightless,
floating, as the presence of God envelops
upon my skin,

I am covered in emotion.

I am present.

Clothed in His smile,
I am here.

Sono a casa,
amongst this vivacity,
this vulnerable vibrancy.

A hurricane of colors
is shimmering, so wildly,
piercing all that's grey.

Here, they live without shields.

The human touch, given freely.
The body, shameless.

> *Tell me, have you ever wanted to pull up the entirety of the world*
> *with your bare hands, holding it close as a kiss on the lips*
> *—like drilling for oil under the surface?*

Swaddle this sand that is clothing the earth
around my warm body;
immerse me in this effervescent vitality.

Resurrect my lungs, my soul, my eyes,
to never stop breathing, feeling, seeing,
with such intensity.

I am embraced by the world,
touching the floor of the sea,
sensing it's ever for me,
blanketed by the ocean
that is sparkling,
mesmerizing.

Here I am twisting,
under the water,

in a kingdom of light,
eyes wide, smiling,
returning to the deeps.

I am swallowing the sun whole.

> *Let it burst open,*
> *all the light within me.*

Unburying depths of courage and intimacy.

I can't stop staring
at the horizon.

The unending edges of this earth
before me.

They are within reach.

This is euphoria.

Eden Is in Our Veins

August 4, 2022
Solanos, Italy
10:47 a.m.

The sky is blending into the sea,
watercolors fusing all around you and me.

The horizon is indistinguishable from air—
look! Heaven and Earth meet!

Never far, never separated,
do not be afraid of what it means to be.

Spill your heart out like this sea!
Endless vastness!
Feel it! Feel all of it!
Feel everything.

Despite everything that shouts
in your flesh and skull,
do not fracture within.

Welcome all of your pieces.
All of life is a gracious gift!

Pain is a privilege;
it means you're alive.

How we can touch God!
How we can hear Him!
Oh, how we can *know* Him!
How can this be?!
His face is so beautiful!

We're reconciled back to the Garden,
all that's been lost is being restored.
What joy it is to be one.

Eden is in our veins when we fall and when we rise.

Simply being
with God—
this is heaven.

God Kissed Me

August 4, 2022
Solanos, Italy
10:59 a.m.

Rejection has constricted my lungs
for far too long,
such an overplayed,
discordant song.

But I watched the stars last night,
looking intently, simply sitting.

When God drew near,
His smile kissed me.

I finally breathed,
warm tears falling.

. . .

I was the woman under the table,
saying the crumbs are enough.

You were waiting for me,
to wrestle and realize my worth.

The Spirit of a Woman

August 4, 2022
Solanos, Italy
3:57 p.m.

The spirit of a woman
is like that of a wild horse.

Unrestrained and unbridled,
a containment of infinities.

Receptive and open,
life penetrates her being,
She is an endless spectrum of colors,
bursting!

There is reason she weeps,
her love, a burning wildness,
untamed, ever overflowing.

Fully integrated,
not contradicting.

She understands
the both, and.

She is fully worthy
to become a full expression—
to live without boundary.

She burns
for the restoration of all things.

Powerful and lowly,
soft and fierce,
whispers and screams,
rooted and soaring,

receptive and open—
a nurturing dichotomy of beauty.

An Essay on Womanhood

She went months only wearing her hair in a ponytail in second grade, because she felt vulnerable and insecure with it down. In middle school, she didn't trust the "girly" girls because they felt inauthentic, insensitive, and mean. But in comparison, a sensitive* tomboy through and through, they reminded her of where she felt she fell short. Observing unsettled insecurity in motherly figures unknowing how to healthily embrace their own feminity; as well as, lacking presence in words and emotions from male figures in her life, she didn't feel worthy. So she compartmentalized it into a defensive state of simply not caring or wanting to have to be or look a certain way—with makeup plastered on her face to be desired. She never saw—what felt like a fight for attention—go anywhere good; so she redirected it. She decided, to hell with it, she would prove herself worthy other ways.

In elementary school, she won in any athletic competition against boys. She hated feeling deemed as "lesser than", just because she was a girl. In the insecurity of her worth, she continually made sure she was better, faster, smarter, stronger. She wasn't going to be rejected further, so she rejected first. She didn't yet know how to feel safe in her intense tenderness, sensitive empathy, unbridled passion and pure feminine expression, so she buried her heart and her femininity to protect herself.

She was me and I know, I am not alone.

*In my observation, I have found, that though tom boys can come off as more "hardened or gritty" they are often much more senssitive, attuned and affected by the layered dynamics around them than the girly girl. Though, this is not to be formalistic and malleable in its subjectivity.

Though, before moving on, I want to state that I am not claiming I have this all "figured out." I simply want to expose light and articulate what I have been studying and observing in our current cultural moment—in my own heart and within the world around me.

In my research, *The Freely Rooted Podcast* stated something that hit me as true: "The majority of time, women don't feel safe to embody the feminine pull in their relationships." I felt this nailed it on the head; as in my own journey and observation around me, I've been learning that *reclaiming safety is the key to unlocking true femininity.*

Think about how many women currently have pepper spray hooked onto their keychains or in their purses. Notice advertisements, look at billboards in broad daylight that are casually endorsing gentlemen's clubs where women are constantly degraded, sexualized, and used for their bodies. The result from this reality fits into one of two extremes.** On one end, you have the woman who has swallowed herself hollow in her pain by solely finding her worth in being sexualized: the playboy bunny. On the other, you have the rage-filled, altogether-independent-from-men, androgynous woman who has built a two-ton concrete wall against her pain. For women, it is this: one seeks attention while losing her own authenticity, in doing all the things culture around her deems as "desirable" in order to "fit in" (literally) or in defense against rejection; one ironically rejects her own femininity, in

** To be noted—these observations are highlighting "ends" on a complex, *unending* spectrum of womanhood. This is a mere scratching of the surface—to the depth of naunce and individual experience within this topic as a whole.

building a wall against it. Both are a result of an immense lack of safety. Both are perverted forms of womanhood.

Being truly, wholly woman is a rebellious thing. So is being truly, wholly man.

I sat in a class once, called "Whole-Hearted Women" led by a dear pastor from Bethel Church named Hayley Braun that is still impacting me to this day.

My heart was burning while she stated, "Unanswered questions create instability. Instability creates insecurity. Insecurity will create competition. And competition kills creativity . . . I realized I had to come to the core questions I had internally and I had to start answering them, otherwise I was going to continue operating out of insecurity and in comparison and that would kill that authentic representation of how God has made me."

The two pendulum swings of womanhood exemplified above are both driven by *unanswered questions.*

At the core root, I believe the question inside every woman is, "Am I worthy?"

The source you can trace back to from any other internal question like tributaries.

"Am I beautiful?" "Am I desirable?" "Am I worth attention, time and pursuit?" "Am I enough?" "Am I too much?" "Am I significant?" "Am I capable?" "Can I be fierce and tender?" "Can I see my dreams come to life?"

"Am I worthy?"

There are many layers to the birthplace of these unanswered questions within us, rooted in both relationship with male and female—mother and father. Though in relation to women and father to son, male passivity might be one of the most prominent iniquities[***] of our day and age because of how it produces unanswered questions. What do I mean by that? Male absence: men stuck in cycles of toxic shame and the fear of inadequacy; limiting belief systems of powerlessness and victimhood causing them to experience poor relationship with ownership and responsibility. This results in a passivity that keeps them emotionally distant, disconnected, and shut down internally. Where, inside their own human fears and vulnerabilities, they find it hard to be emotionally present to their own hearts; much less emotionally aware of the effects on the hearts of those around them. Hiding where they are made to conquer.

Men are made to speak identity into chaos.

Think about how one of the first things God had Adam do was name the animals. Men are made to call out identity with their presence and voice.

When men are living inside passivity, compartmentilizing and shoving aside, lacking vulnerablity, detached, on cruise control—not fully trusting in their own adequacy or being aware of the depth of impact of their presence, voice, and actions—their own absence internally leaves voids of silence outwardly where they were made to call out identity.

[***]Etymologically iniquity means "twisted and distorted." Anything that is outside of God's original intention of design.

This is just a layer inside many of the effect of unanswered questions, for passivity in men comes from their own unanswered questions internally—just as for women, it's where we see the predominent iniquities of control, rage, and independence.

While men are fashioned to be protectors and providers, women are fashioned to be receptive and open like a flower in bloom. Except, when not dealt with, the effect of these core unanswered questions is a woman who feels unsafe: hardened; harsh; hustle-bent; angry from the absence of pure male leadership, communication, covering, presence, and protection. You have women in unhealthy, emotional defensive states with tears in their eyes and gritted jaws, writing sentences like this at a feminine exhibit at the British Museum: "No longer wanting equality alone but wanting revenge for the mistreatment of womanhood. It's a rage that gets stuck at the back of your throat." Though the mistreatment is valid, rage is never righteous. For at its core, it is not power but fear. The deep feeling of being unsafe. This causes the dysfunctional effect of women becoming hyper-independent, running their bodies to the ground in the pursuit of trying to be enough. Operating out of insecurity, trying to answer the core questions internally. Usually living rigid inside an unhealthy relationship with help; the very protection and provision they are longing for. Sometimes, even to the point of simply rolling their eyes at doors being opened for them. As well as women not honoring their cyclical being, shut down to their creativity and nurture—*consumptive, better, harder, faster.*

Hear me; I'm not pinning the problem on men. As the unhealthiness of control, rage and independence inside a women is just as much a part of the layered cause and effect of male passivity. There is such compassion in my heart for men who have experienced the harsh, seemingly irrational, hypercritical, "overly emotional", abandoned woman in pain—especially when from their own mother figures. I can only imagine how this has caused similar distrust in their own hearts toward women, leading them to the pattern of dissociation and withdrawal—or on the other side of a man's pendulum swing—distorts conquer with control. Because it is all just too confusing and overwhelming, having left them feeling shame and unsafe themselves since they were little boys.

Before I move on further, as the woman writing this, who has also been harsh and hypercritical in moments—I want to apologize to any man reading this who has experienced this from women. You are worth feeling safe just as much as we are and I am sorry for any way a woman has made you feel small and unsafe inside her own pain.

Women need men, just as men need women, to thrive. Again, my heart is to expose a juxtaposed reality beneath the surface and expand our compassion toward ourselves as well as the opposite sex. It is a both, and. There is ownership on both ends. The issue is cause and effect, and we're both missing the mark because of pain.

So what does healing look like? It is fascinating and telling how suppression and control is the most primary way society has tried to silence women. Look at the Middle East to the 1950's, corrupt theological views on women preaching and teaching, grotesquely how women are to "submit" to men, any fight for women's rights or equity, Barbie ("Just get back in the box."), and on and on and on.

Women are meant to be wild and unconfined—grounded in nature, whimiscal and as free as the wind, fluid and vast as the ocean—like a lung fully inhaling and exhaling, providing life itself. Women need space, safety, and security to embody the multi-layered aspects of feminity. Though most only experience confinement and imperilment in society—including within some of our closet relationships.

Not knowing how to regulate this, women experience a state of adrenaline that disconnects them from their proliferative core of nurture. For men, passivity can cause apathy: a sluggish, aloof, avoidant state. Where for women, the effect is usually the opposite. Like static electricity, they develop a hyper-hurried, hyper-fixated, hypercritical internal state. Here is where the issue of body image for women can emerge. At its root, it is a control issue. A woman develops tunnel vision toward herself. As the world feels out of control around her, she makes a reach for control—for information, for analyzation, for explanation, for revenge—to try to understand what feels disoriented and rejected within her. But women are just waiting and aching for permission and safety to sink into the expansiveness of feminitiy.

So what do we do with this? We yield to love. We, men and women, take ownership over the places inside of us where we have contributed to the dysfunctional loop of the cause and effect.

As women, we choose to courageously face the core questions inside ourselves and begin letting love answer them. We choose to heal, bravely doing the internal work required to become deeply aware—no longer operating out of familiar driving systems of rejection, abandonment, and insecurity that are marring the authenticity we were made to carry.

We choose forgiveness. We rage against the supression and control by surrending the need for revenge—for the bitter ache for revenge is suppression itself. We endure the pain without retaliation and fight against injustice by doing the brave work to unravel out of all internal suppression. We relinquish control and open up our clenched fists of self-protection. We surrender our walls and we choose compassion. We continually unlearn these patterns built by pain and learn the freeing truths of our Creator's way, the fullness of His intent. As women, we courageously choose to unravel out of hiddenness and areas of self-abandonment. With further bravery, reconnecting to and rescuing the little girl inside us who doesn't feel safe. We choose to step out of defense and into the radical, vulnerable gift of the wildness and liberty of womanhood. We allow our full selves to be seen, restoring trust with ourselves internally—owning our voices and the fullness of our expression. Breaking off the restraints of comparison and competition, locking arms together with the gift of unity, championing each other to become completely unbridled and liberated in each of our diverse, unique, authentic expressions.

In our innate nature, women possess a knowledge of life itself that makes the earth burn and turn on its axis. Radically resilient, like how a flower blooms faithfully through the seasons, not just in a blink of a moment, women crave slowness to freely become. Made to be fully unsurpressed and uncontrolled—inside themselves—delivering the world from supression and control around them. Providing and unveiling the awe-striking divergent spectrum, fire and delicate beauty of life itself.

The wholehearted woman—she is a giver and sustainer of life. She is angry about injustice but not filled with rage. She fights for the restoration of all things by becoming restored herself. She ceases the striving to regain power where it felt stripped—she is no longer vying against men. Owning her own voice; she tells the truth while dignifying them. She craves growth. She presses into healing. She knows the only way to resolve anger is through acceptance— fully acknowledging the places of pain she was never meant to be dealt with—forgiving quickly, deeply, and often. She is proliferative at the core, there is a desire to grow the world outside of herself through care and nurture. She nourishes herself and everything around her. She knits her own and other communities together. She has deep trust in the provision and beauty of life. She is deeply acquainted with surrender and sacrifice. She is a leader and a learner. She is at rest; her worth and intrinsic value have nothing to do with responses from men or others. She is an innate problem solver, deeply engaged with creativity, and knows there are many answers to solve an issue. She sees all angles. She carries the missing piece within men; she is deeply needed and valued. She is expansive. She has permission to become a full expression. She is worth time, attention, energy, and work. She celebrates without comparison. She doesn't easily give up. She asks hard questions and doesn't settle for half-hearted answers. She practices honesty and offers empathy. She is tuned into her body with kindness and acceptance. She knows she is made to hold the fullness of life. She grieves without losing hope. She seeks wisdom and receives the space to learn. She is soft, tenaciously open, extremely resilient, and wildly receptive to life. She carries the very essence of beauty, power, creativity, wonder, and whimsy. She is fully, infinitely worthy.

Women are meant to be given unending space to experience the containment of these infinities. All of the both, ands, with no fences. The soft and fierce. Powerful and humble. Tender and gracious. Quiet and loud. Whispers and screams. Shallow water and deep. Tears and laughter. Tender toward what's right and angry toward what's wrong. Flexible and intentional. Tired and awake. Discerning and forgiving. Strong and wise. Grit and honesty. Able to listen and willing to speak. Protects and is protected. She is captivating. She is a dichotomy of beauty.

In her, there is no more defense. No more proving. No more fighting. No more striving to be enough. No more competition with the masculine. No more state of resistance but a state of trust. No more reactiveness but responsiveness. No more confined boxes. No more black and white state of thinking, but filled with the full spectrum of every color within herself. No more threat. No more fear. She is receptive and open. She is soft, powerful and safe within herself. She is unrestrained and unbridled. She is wholeheartedly woman.

She is love embodied. She is iridescent.

"The cost of anything is the amount of life you exchange for it."
—Henry David Thoreau

The Cost

For Amy, from our conversation at dinner in Italy

August 6, 2022
On the plane to Paris
8:28 p.m.

We strip life by trying to cheat it,
rocks skipping across the surface,
"beware the barrenness of business."[*]

Afraid of the ocean deep, not realizing
the shallow end is what's terrifying.

Constricting boxes,
labeled with Sharpie!
Their names,
comfort and avoidance.

By seeking for loopholes from pain,
we become puppets with strings,
religiously shouting at each other to walk on water!
In a busy ache to stay above the surface

[*] "Beware the barrenness of business" is a quote from the brilliant Amy Alexander

to not experience the "negative",
not understanding, never understanding—
that's not what faith is.
So yield, surrender to the depths you ignore
to learn how to truly float upwards,
rising completely unafraid,
finding all of life—our hearts,
iridescent,
below the surface,
just waiting
for the light to fully absorb.

Embrace the waves of life without fear,
faith is in the reaching out of your hand.

Failure is stagnancy, not sinking.

Perhaps the treasure you are seeking
has been waiting there all along,
beneath your capsized ego,
where you hear Him in the dark night say,
"Did you not know it was me?"

Inside of us, in the fold of the page
where it's hardest to read,
when it's most difficult to see
—amongst the grey,
where touch, a hand on your cheek,

another's eyes, another's loving voice,
is found in the sinking deep,
in the inviting, where you awake,
just under the surface,
delivered out of self-preserving.

Hear Jesus ask, oh!
The loving kindness of question!

In pain He shouts,
in joy He whispers.

"Did you not know it was me?"
The ghost out on the choppy sea.
The man so near
in all of the questions.
Burning. Aching. Longing.

Your ego doesn't want to die!
But come and see!

Convenience is what's costly.

The man who steals ultimately steals
the most from himself.

The man who compartmentalizes himself from pain
ultimately writhes in it.

For what is it worth?

To exchange false comfort for the sobriety of your soul
—the reality of what it means to be whole.

Life or death, this is the cost.

Tug apart strings of control that tether your soul,
discover the exquisite risk of awakening.

Come a little deeper;
the waters are inviting.

In the basin of the human soul
is the presence of Adonai
on its storm-tossed waters,
hovering, revealing.

...

Don't be afraid
of this wild mystery.

His will,
To unite everything.

Where hope is a light,
from the inside, never waning.

Humility & Abounding

August 7, 2022
Paris, France
10:19 a.m.

Breathing in deep, looking ahead, inside a dream,
surrounded by thousands of years of reformation,
of art, of hearts—so passionately alive,
so honest that it has completely shaped history.

Let it move me,
a dandelion in the wind,
a wish, bend me.

God, let this city teach me
how to be true through and through.

To agree with the intentional and unique significance within.
Like the exquisite details reflected inside its architecture,
this city's very blueprint,
calling out to us off the walls,
knocking on all of *ours*,
reminding us of the importance of our fingerprints.

To come forward, to fully emerge, to be utterly undignified,
unafraid and unhindered—
lowly, humble, so authentic, so honest, so pure—

our hearts made to be like paint splattered on a canvas,
expressing freely, no longer fearing to be fully seen,
for all that is innocent at the core,
the rushing array of color inside
—no longer watered down—
ever radiant, ever potent,
pure, pure, pure.

Cobblestones, terraces,
swarming diversity,
Monet's voice whispering.
My bones reverberating,
longing, as I'm finding
this *beauty is exposing*
the things I've been holding back,
hiding.

Knowing, that what's inside is worth it,
to spill out, even at the fray.

This city is holding me inside a meek feeling,
of being surrounded by awe-striking mountains,
or gazing upon the vastness of the Milky Way,
a reminding—*there's deep purpose in being alive.*

Let this city unearth my heart's gift to do the same.

Let this gift of abounding clothe me in the reverence of humility.

Creativity is what makes us,
reflects us.

Lord, let it read me like Braille,
especially where the shadows lie.

Where we all cover the words of our hearts in our journals
with our hands when people draw near in open spaces so they
can't fully read.

—where we're all just asking,

could we break these bones
'til they're better?

The ache, the question—
am I enough? Do you see me?

How long
can one carry all this armor?

Would an ocean of tears fall—
like the jam I dropped
on the earth this morning—
for holding back?

No longer just people-pleasing, gritting,
"*Desolé! Desolé!*"

Could I stop saying
sorry—
for spilling?

To be unapologetic
—a full expression,
like the art in this city.

Creativity is what makes us,
reflects us.

Lord, let its honest expression
teach me.

Shouldering this grandiosity,
I see myself more acutely,
and there are many places
where I am sorry
for playing hide and seek,
inside lack, making others fight to see me
—wrestling past all my wounds, layers, and walls.

Lord, let the abounding clothe me in humility.

Help me to spill out abundantly,
no longer self-protecting,
fully bleeding, relentless in love and *fully exposed*
—true, naked, and unashamed.

Fully discovered and settled,
inside the covering of the exposure of vulnerability.

This is where I am learning,
and unlearning.

And where I pray
I always will be
continually unraveling.

Lord, clothe me
in humility and abounding.

Here,
I hear you fully now when you say,

"I need you to bleed for me."

Help me to trust your love,
to let mine spill without shields,
without fear,
unrestrained from the depths of me.

Help us all,
to let love cost us,
in every fiber of our being
—our being, that is more abundant,
even so much more
than the thousands of years of richness held within the entirety of this city.

Because like the Mona Lisa,
you and I
are worth going to the ends of the earth for,
just to be seen.

Illuminating: A Soliloquy

August 8, 2022
Gillian & Eddy's House
Antrim, Ireland
5:34 p.m.

"*Is this real?*"
Whispers under the breath,
gratefulness so pure it has to expand.
A soliloquy.

The sun is shining through
200-year-old white-paneled windows,
kissing cherry hardwood floors,
dancing on the keys of a mahogany piano.

Bookshelves lining the walls,
the dusty rose-petal curtains
are glimmering, the dust
particles flickering,
in the light.

History. Presence.
Here. I am here.

My heart—
a slow river, widening,

steady, pulsating, living.

In the stillness,
I am feeling.

"*Wow, I've always longed for this.*"

And don't we all
ache just to be truly whole,
tasting desires fulfilled,
to be fully present,
to carry legacy,
like this house.

Don't we all just long
to return to origin,
to be fully connected,
body, mind, spirit, and soul?

To be fully aware,
swimming in the gift of kindness,
our souls tethered,
a feeling of comfort,
like a weighted blanket,
elixir, tears of joy on our cheeks.
Guttural laughter, so much so

it hurts our bellies.

Courage, forever taking us upstream.
For brevity to say exactly the things we mean.

Like, I love you, I love you deeply.

For bravery to go after our dreams,
without fear of limitation.

Most of all, for humility.

Grace to truly see,
to see rightly.

Faith to believe,
this is where light elucidates—
everything.

"I want to see your face, Lord.
Help me, I have to know you deeper."

I am a child catching fireflies in my backyard.
I am the Mason jar, they are inside of me,
a buzz of light! Exploding!

Suddenly, I am seven again,

looking at the stuffed Irish frog that sat
on my bookshelf next to Harry Potter—
the one my godmother sewed for me.

With her hands. She did that for me.
I am realizing—I've always been carried.

I am awakening.
I am present.
I am dreaming.
I am remembering.

I am bending,
amongst my friends—the trees—
searching for four-leaf clovers in the untamed grass
of Oklahoma. Did I ever find them? No.

Everyone told me they weren't there.

But still, I kept looking, and here,
at twenty-seven, they found me.

"Am I so lucky?
Or was it that I always believed?"

All is—
Illuminating.

Cigarettes & Fig Trees

August 8, 2022
Journey Community Church
Antrim, Ireland
11:23 p.m.

In the rearview mirror there are
foreign, tired-bright wide eyes.

Even here, across time zones,
you still circumnavigate my mind.

When will it all stop hurting?

Maybe I should stop,
stopping the bleeding
until I'm steam rising
from a pour-over
in the morning—
with new mercy.

> Cappuccinos and scones.
> Cigarettes and fig trees.

Where can I grow
to be enough for you?
In the blur,

I just keep asking.

>*This didn't start with you,*
>only now fully exposed,
>in the roots,
>under the fig leaves,
>where my mind has been circling,
>digging, in search of an olive branch
>—uprooting.

Of course I'd deny it,
snow globe realities
are easier on the mind.

>Though, if I'm being honest,
>lately my tongue,
>is a knife—carving
>the tiny gap in my
>front teeth.

I never noticed
this 'til now—insecurity.

>Could I ripen,
>fall off green branches

and become earth again?

Could we rewind and retry this,
all over again?

We can pick through my mistakes,
how I took a crow bar to the parts of your heart
within reach, yet a thousand miles away.

You'll see me crying,
inside the tears reflected in your eyes
—ensuing a perpetual silence.

At the end of the day,
could we all just be
stripped down,
dust to dust,
deep to deep.

Reconnected,
accepted in the garden,
as is
—loving wholeheartedly.

Hearts no longer breaking,
bathing within reconciliation,
holding each other's face,

in the palm of our hands,
only seeing the miraculous
—this,
is the longing.

These veins
under my jaw
that clench
when I sleep
are stems of flowers
amidst the concrete—
aching against, yet growing,
breaking through,
finding a way,
tended to,
by the Gardener's mercy.

Could I know that
they're already blooming,
innately carrying beauty that's worthy.
Holy, a woman worth choosing
—beholding.

> And when will I know I'm enough?
> When gravity is no longer a law to my heart and soul
> —ascending.

"*Come near,*" He just keeps on whispering,
ever, ever so sweetly
—tethering me in, *healing.*

> Songs, laughs, cries
> you and I,
> in all our pieces and sighs.

We're all one,
heartbreakingly beautiful
—humanity.

> *I see myself,*
> *when I see you.*

Scared.
Brave.
Hurting.
Healing.
Trying.
Fighting.
Loving.

Smoking cigarettes,
under fig trees.

If Just for a Moment

August 9, 2022
Crosskeys Pub
Northern Ireland, UK
10:33 p.m.

Joy moves like blood—
pounding, echoing inside of me,
reminding me that it's true:
what we hold dear
can heal the world.

I couldn't explain what I felt in the moment,
something so pure, beyond words,
but my quivering smile and unrecoverable tears
told me it was everything—
a glimpse of eternity.

Irish violin strings
turned the room
into a wide-open field
where I am washed in innocence,
with wide eyes filled with wonder.

Their sound, like a trumpet call to awaken—
life is exploding, colors are flooding everything.

We were without fear,
infinitely alive,
if just for a moment.

Held within the symphony
of the miraculous gift of being.

And as I leave,
the man at the bar smiles
and says,
"I wish all the best to you,
all your days,"
and I never felt
more like he really, truly meant it.

If just for a moment,
I swear,
we experienced
the infinite.

Praying Women Change History

August 10, 2022
Journey Community Church
Antrim, Northern Ireland
11:50 p.m.

Presence,
hot liquid love,
sears my chest;
soft tears
fall like rain on a windshield.

My friends are calling on heaven,
when suddenly, I see His face.

Then further,
something I've yet to see,
His eyes are diamonds!

In every single angle,
such reverent purity!

I am seeing so clearly,
how He is so gloriously
holy.

Unable to even move

—laid out prostrate on the floor,
overwhelmed by
fear and trembling.

We are together,
no competition,
no comparison
—unity.

Twelve of us
are on our knees
in this empty loft
above the sanctuary.

This is where
praying women
change history.

Hot Tears

August 11, 2022
Shane's Castle
Northern Ireland, UK
8:30 p.m.

Here comes the glory,
sweeping through the room,
the dam in my chest
suddenly bursting
—hot tears.

Jesus's face, illuminating.
His amber-green eyes,
His eyes, *my very favorite thing,*
beholding.

I see Him;
He is so beautiful
it's terrifying.

I'm a wild horse in an endless field,
no longer holding myself together.

Fully unbridled.

Fully beside myself,
in love.

Process

August 11, 2022
Shane's Castle
Northern Ireland, UK
8:50 p.m.

My dear friend is longing for healing,
on a midnight moonlit Northern Ireland beach.

We wade into the ocean of question and mystery.

She is naked, sinking deep in faith
amidst painful realities, believing for healing.

It's been a lifetime I've prayed,
my mom has yet to be healed.

I watched my friend go into this ocean alone,
I didn't unclothe myself here.

Hot tears

now soak my face
as I lay down to sleep.

If I could go back—
instead of holding myself together,

guarded in self-protection,
I would have stepped under those waters,

into the ocean inside of me,
that I was mad at and afraid of,
lonely.

This is where tonight,
I am sorry.

We're all in the process of healing,
though I'm done with self-preserving.

Lowly

August 12, 2022
Shane's Castle
Northern Ireland, UK
12:00 a.m.

Faith apprehends,
and faith lets go.

So come,
there is a door so low—
you must crawl through.

It's where He hides us in the cleft of the rock;
the door to life,
the wound in His side.

For the only way to see Him
is from the inside.

There is the unveiling, look!
Your eyes are adjusting to the glorious light!

There is a Man waiting on the other side,
so pure, He offers to wash you.

He is bent over alone, weeping, interceding,

every fiber of your heart is burning.

There is a bucket of water and a sponge.
You long to comfort Him; He is so meek,
so lowly.

You grab it and begin washing His feet,
just to be able to do anything.

He grabs your chin, lifts it,
you can now see Him softly smiling.

Glossy tears are in His green eyes,
flushed with passion.

Few share in His suffering.

Your eyes can't look away
as the veil of the heart
is violently torn to pieces,
melting internally the stone of
pride and self-sufficiency.

Searing awareness.

Your eyes now see everything,
a mosaic of holy mystery.

You are now weeping uncontrollably,
bent over alone—where letting go
is a kind of heaven.

With this vulnerable Man
whose name is
Humility.

Clothed in Majesty.

Conviction

August 13, 2022
Journey Community Church
Antrim, Northern Ireland
11:46 p.m.

Soften my edges,
all the things that callous
me from you.

Help me to stay in the river,
fully submerged under the water of your voice,
making contact with the fullness of reality,
ever present to truth.

Have mercy,
convict me from hardening,
pour fire on the self-inflicting separation of unbelief.

For a hard heart is rebellion,
its question is "Where is the Lord?"

Though it was always us that left,
never Him.

Look back,
repent.

Draw near.

There is the Lord.
Never distant.

"I am still every age that I have been. Because I was once a child, I am always a child. Because I was once a searching adolescent, given to moods and ecstasies, these are still part of me, and always will be . . . this does not mean that I ought to be trapped or enclosed in any of these ages . . . the delayed adolescent, the childish adult, but that they are in me to be drawn on; to forget is a form a suicide . . . far too many people misunderstand what putting away childish things mean and think that forgetting what it is like to think and feel and touch and smell and taste and see and hear like a three-year-old or a twenty-three-year-old means being grownup. When I'm with these people, I, like the kid, feel that if this is what it means to be a grown-up, then I don't ever want to be one. Instead of which, if I retain a child's awareness and joy and *be* fifty-one, then I will really learn what it means to be grown up."
—Madeleine L'Engle

All That We Carry

August 14, 2022
Shane's Castle
Northern Ireland, UK
3:06 p.m.

We are the sum total of our past,
every age of ourselves, within us.

We hold our conflicts in our minds,
where our memories reside.

Life is difficult;
we lose that which we love.

We wish things would have never happened,
we wish we could have more time.

We hope to never have to say goodbye.

We hold onto anger because we feel
we have some sort of right.

Because control is what we long for;
what cannot be understood
terrifies the mind.

But control itself is impossible,
though we try.

We bury ourselves,
starting in sandpits as a kid,
little shovels of our emotions,
down deeper and deeper still.

Forgetting what we knew
when we were young,
that the messy and miry places
were beautiful to hold.

Creating in the mud,
unafraid of

all that we carry.

Now we think maybe
the more we can suppress,
the more control we'll feel.

As the axis of the world
spins on its head,
and we pretend,
disconnected from what's real.

We say we're okay, we're healed,
but we're lying through our teeth.

Looking for peace
that's authentic,
but our legs are paddling,
like a duck's under the sea.

We're scared to look at the pain, the voids inside,
we're frightened of what will happen if we do.
Though, what is it that is so alarming about honesty,
about truth?

> *Can you imagine saying what you really think?*
> *The horror of saying what you might mean?*
> *Tell us where you are wrestling,*
> *you'll find a crowd waiting.*

And we believe triggers mean we need more healing,
as if "maturity" is to not be affected
—who taught us this?

Jesus wept.
Have we forgotten childlikeness?

I laughed too,
having found light swimming through all the blinds,
inside of me—at every age,

all the rooms fully alive,
then went on weeping.
If you have yet to find yourself hysterical,
then keep looking.

Pain is a teacher,
not our enemy.

There are no negative feelings,
they just are

even more,
all are good,

defibrillators of the heart.

You don't judge an emotion,
you feel it, all of it.

You heal a relationship—
with self, with God, with others—
you rescue a life.

Mend the gaps and fractures
by being painfully soft,
brutally honest,
always, continually

asking for help,
then accepting it.

For if we can't accept to die to self—to die at all,
we can't accept to live.

So walk through the valley of the shadow of death,
with His rod and His staff,
to know we really can fear no evil,
feasting on communion,
together at the table.

And the answer to it all,
in the beginning and the end—

surrender.

*Childishness is different from childlikeness. *It's actually the opposite.* Childishness is self absorption—unable to see beyond the self. Childlikeness is rooted in maturity inside the gift of wonder: the ability to lose one's own dignity, shedding the tunneled vision inside the seriousness of the ego and seeing all of life, self and others in a surrendered, incredibly humbling and awe-striking full spectrum.

———————

Triggers will never go away; they are a beautiful part of the human experience. They are an invitation.

Our goal is to not outgrow them but grow inward, becoming softer, more mailable. We can never truly grow if we continue to relate to triggers/our humanity with shame. Love is the only thing that transforms.

We have a choice. We can choose to dissociate, to be swallowed in shame, or we can choose to grow inward into sobriety and connection. Making contact with the full reality of ourselves and our experience like a child—deeply present and authentic without masks—is the work of humility. Living without shadow or fracture, fully connected, is what it means to walk in the divinity of being an apprentice to Jesus.

Experiencing connection and acceptance within ourselves, in our pain, is like Windex to the soul. It's where the fog lifts and we begin to see clearly. This is where we are filled with peace, internal stillness—our minds becoming grounded and aware. This is the path of true maturity.

wake up
wake up
wake up

A Shattered Hourglass

August 17, 2022
Ozone Coffee Roasters
London, UK
1:56 p.m.

It is safe to dream.
Even when
disappointment
festers in the gap between
expectation and reality.

Those places where
there is a shattered hourglass of time at your feet,
though *urgency is a myth,*
do not submit to it.

Continue to risk with such fire and courage
that it doesn't make sense.

Again and again,
shatter the hourglass within.

"No longer wanting equality alone but wanting revenge
for the mistreatment of womanhood. It's a rage that gets
stuck at the back of your throat."

—I studied a woman who wrote this on the wall at the British
Museum on feminine power.

"I wish I were a girl again, half savage, hardy and free."
—Emily Brontë

Woman

A response to the woman writing on the wall,
I watched you with tears in my eyes.

August 18, 2022
The British Museum
London, UK
5:55 p.m.

Men are without a rib, women carry this.
We are needed, at the side.

Though, yes,
we've been controlled into submissiveness.

We're red. With rage.

But rage is never power,
it is fear.

An ache to regain control,
where it's felt stripped,
lost inside a feeling of exhausting helplessness.

An experience, valid, one that I know.

Though, *independence from one another
is demonic.*

Man and Woman
are made for the other.

I hear your cries—
what does it mean to be fully woman?!

I answer this:
In laying down your need for vindication.

Surrender
is where true power is.

Unrestrained, unconditional love,
an untamed savage force that breaks through every false prison.

Note,
how when you are receptive and open,
unguarded and unshielded,
you can see a rainbow,
reflecting the full spectrum,
wholly unsuppressed within you.

How truth is discovered
when the light is allowed to shine through!

Woman.

She is an array of multifaceted,
uncontainable infinities of color,
like fluid light inside a prism,
a bouquet of wildflowers,
made to be seen and cherished,
at every angle.

Forever worthy to bloom,
to grow, to become,
entirely safe, cared for,
carrying all of her expression,
unhidden and true.

Woman.

She is the full spectrum of light
You cannot contain her—life-giving radiance,
awakening, to help you see,
all that is, beauty.

She is iridescent.

No Flaw or Weakness

August 20, 2022
Eastcote, West London
10:28 p.m.

The heart
seems to always get caught
in the throat;
shallow breaths,
emotions that we sugarcoat.

Would we burn all the old masks,
not knowing where the next steps
take us, as it should be—
explorers of mystery,
living in divine tension,
listeners to the sea,
to the depths of the heart,
the shore of the soul,
that holds too great
a promise to be ignored,
one that returns us back home.

Take a moment,
inhale, deep breaths,
a settled stillness,
making visible the wind.

Feel,
a hand extended,
laid open,
without judgment,
making visible love.

Even before the Fall,
it wasn't good for man to be alone.

Could we be courageous enough
to look through the folds
of every cry and meet each other
at the horizons of our souls?

To be human is to need;
this is not—and has never been—
flaw or weakness.

In need, we are whole.

This is what it means to become.

You come
into being.

Scary close,
no longer

afraid of being fully seen.

Take off the fig leaves.

Cut Me Like a Rose

A memory, originally written at Mt. Lassen National Park

August 21, 2022
Grind Coffee Shop
London, UK
1:09 p.m.

I'm staring out past the windows,
you

cut me like a rose,
delicate and susceptible,
better than before.

I didn't tell you,
but I was falling in love.

Diamonds for Eyes
A prayer

Grind Coffee Shop
August 21, 2022
1:24 p.m.

Your nearness is my good.

Yeshua,
further open my eyes.

I cannot,
without your light.

I am leaning, bleeding, spilling.
Moving all my truth toward you.

Here help me to see
every single aspect of you—
bind and unveil,
where your body tore everything,
that tries to separate me in two.

Deliver me,
everywhere that I am blind,
for you have shown me,

you have diamonds for eyes.

I ache to discover
all there is of you.

Oh Lord, reveal,
open my heart to see every facet of truth!

Help me to see in every angle
everything I cannot
and have not yet,
like you,
with the purity of a raw cut diamond.

I am
needy.

I just have to have all of you,
filling all the space in between,
with the richness of your glory.

Circumnavigate

August 22, 2022
On the train to Manchester
Stoke-on-Trent, UK
12:31 p.m.

There are two extremes to avoidance:
absorb or distract.

Circumnavigate the void you feel,
or surrender to the inevitability of pain,
letting go inside all its waves,
to find the deep end—
where joy becomes real.

Pain and fear will not overtake you;
it puffs itself up but only resides
in the shallow end—

so go lower, lower still.

Love Is a Circle

August 23, 2022
Foundation Coffee House
Manchester, UK
2:39 p.m.

A rain drop,
a steering wheel, a wheel at all,
a windmill.

The ballpoint of a pen,
a bullseye, the end of a dart within.

A doorknob,
a pebble falling into a still pond.

Its rippling, its sound,
vibrating, echoing
spherically,
like the cells
—the core makeup
within us all!

An unseen tissue that holds everything!

Ecosystems,
history,

economics,
condensation,
precipitation,
evaporation,
natural cycles,
within,
all the cycles we make!

Your iris, a round mirror,
all the circles where we see!

Inside and inside,
layer after layer,
a Venn diagram,
where we meet!

Look! Heaven is not so hidden!
In Him, we live and move and have our being!

Love is a circle,
never ending.

Inside you and me,
with no end or beginning.

No break,
no pause,
no in-between,
continuous,
forever ongoing
—infinity.

Love is a circle.

Omnipotent,
omnipresent.

All around and within us,
surrounding.

To the very atomic proof,
held within quantum physics.

Love is
always with us.

Forever unconditional,
forever unceasing.

Theater of Dreams

August 24, 2022
Takk Coffee
Manchester, UK
2:11 p.m.

The screech of the Tube,
waking you from sleep.
Drunk, glazed-eyed teenagers
rushing in, chuckling,
tripping, saying,
"Sorry, mate, sorry."

You still think of them
and how they are doing.

In a packed market
a baby cries,
a mother bends
to breastfeed—

a hero daily.

Hues of pastels:
olive green, pink, and blue
paired with exposed brick and stone.

The sound of jackhammers,
city workers clean the pavements.
Yet, stillness: the clouds are barely moving,
hearty accents share melodies,
fog rests just over the buildings,
slow and still, as if calling out to us,
levitating, *waiting.*

Walking for miles without noticing,
            (selah, contentment)
blue eyes, another cigarette to the lips,
the haze swirling into a red beard,
a Guinness pouring, the gentle
move of a hand across the table
onto another's arm—

we're always reaching.

Apple crumble with new friends,
discussing global racism,
and what we do with it.

Revelation requires responsibility,
talk about it.

80,000 fans in a theater of dreams:
grandparents, mothers, fathers,

sons and daughters,
rich and poor and in-between,
white, Southeast Asian, Arab,
African, Pakistani.
A rush of wonder swells from the invisible,
that which is most tangible,
as if all these sounds, moments,
longings, shared fears,
emotions, all of humanity,
the colors of the world,
are surrendering at once
to the glory of unity.

And at the end of the day
we are for each other.
More than anything.

We say bless you
as we sneeze,
we hold hands,
we ask "How are you doing?"
"Are you okay?"
we declare goodness,
inside each shared laugh,
we think of each other,
as we all lay our heads to sleep
with kindness and care,

so innate, so evident,
grinning, after every coffee order,
saying, "Cheers, mate."

We're all just living with dreamers,
in a theater of dreams.

Like branches on a tree, individually
we're all each other's stories.

A Kite in the Sky

August 24, 2022
Regents Park
London, UK
7:23 p.m.

My bare feet are resting against this dry grass,
eyes smiling, arms sprawled under my head
with my back held up by the earth.
I'm alone, but not at all,
closeness surrounds me,
it surrounds us always.

Serenely listening to the laughs of a group
of boys playing football beside me,
then further on in front of me,
watching a child
flying a kite in the sky

and I've often thought
how I could have missed this,
how I could have chosen security
instead of risk.

How, before coming, I was filled with anxiety—
something I don't mention as often as I should.

How even sometimes without me thinking,
it burns down my back like ants crawling.
I never mean to choose it,
it's been since I was a kid.
50 mg is beside my bed,
I'm processing it.

Ever so sensitive,
the vulnerability of life
allures me and terrifies me all at once,
but I have to taste it—draw all its marrow out at the core,
for I know that I know,
bravery to touch its depths,
will continually help me see further
outside of myself, discovering the more.

How, unlike some who run to avoid,
it would have been
easier for me
to stay than go, how—
sometimes this longing for self-preservation haunts me.

How every day requires bravery,
in all its forms.

To be honest, to face ourselves,
to say what we need to say,

to be kind, to repent, to be noble and true.

Amongst it all, daily, I have found bravery
to be the most loyal and protective friend,

shielding me from
that which wants to steal
my voice, my hope, my love,
my vulnerable innocence and purity.

How bravery guides us toward
that which scares us, hinders us most.

But it's there, lowered at the walls
—peering over the edges within us,
with our legs shaking—
that holds the greatest reward.

Adventure is a kite,
seeing everything from above,
held in the hands of a child, yielded fully,
compelled by the wind of love.

I want to be there,
one with the bravery of childlikeness.

So I rented a car to drive in London
so I could immerse myself in the city,

and others said, "Whoa, you're brave,"
but I didn't understand it fully.

It was only like flying a kite in the sky.
Whimsically running, laughing,
tripping, falling until
it all takes off flying,
up, up, up, high!

How much do we not,
by masquerading fear with wisdom?

do we not risk,
do we not explore,
do we not learn,
do we not see,
do we not grow,
do we not love,
do we not feel,
do we not even try,

because of fear—
fear of the very things,
the most vulnerable things,
we long for the most.

The whimsy of intimacy,
the feeling of being truly known,

something so real
—excruciatingly close,
the rush of romance,
the awakening of adventure,
the liberation of honesty,
the depths of joy and acceptance,
that can only be carved out through certain fires of grief.

Oh, how bravery
has been such a dear, dear friend to me;
I will never grow tired of its trustworthy whimsy.

Like this kite that I am watching,
held in the hands of a child,
relentlessly soaring.

stay awake
stay awake
stay awake

We Will Endure

August 25, 2022
On the plane to Charlotte
1:54 p.m.

Draw on the memorial stones
of faithfulness.

Goodness is assured.

By His Spirit,
we will endure.

The Returning

August 25, 2022
The plane home to Oklahoma
9:17 p.m.

The horizon is giving way to the night,
burnt red fading to blood orange,
searing opulent indigo, swimming into
a sea of dark and darker still,
brilliant bold, royal navy blue.

Oh, this blood-transfusion sky,
shining like a lighthouse
against silhouetted clouds,

shows me how the light, too,
silhouettes all I must return to.

Outlining what matters most,
what calls me. Truth that never leaves,
that pursues me, like hope drenching mundanity
—like clouds when they all go pink.

It's true, we only seem to see this best
in certain unusual angles,
like where I sit right now,
high above the clouds

—in the twilight, in the waiting,
the silence of the in-between,
when the sun fades completely,
in moments of the dark nights of our souls,
where we experience
such severe, beautiful mercy.

When a new dawn is so close
it shadows everything
—a loving, purifying fire,
trust built in faithfulness's fidelity.

And like this plane,
may we press onward
over the horizon—ascending to the heavens,
never letting our spirits wain,
through every long, long night,

we must not shrink back

in the suffering, the disillusionment, the longing,
we must persevere, violently raging against the selfishness of
apathy—

for the igniting reality and depths of love!

For it burns, burns, burns—wildly!

Blazing at the cusp of us
in our internal skies,
blazing throughout every night

this love in us, this love!
that is truer than anything.

> *Alone,*
> *we can never grasp it completely,*
> *but together we will see it entirely.*

So if you really want love,
and to love unrestrained,
yielding wholeheartedly,
without condition,
your only option
is to look at yourself,
squarely and deeply,
then surrender completely.

Then you will see Him

—The Light!

Then you will see everything.

In every awe-striking angle,

like a giddy child,
reaching for a translucent bubble
floating in the air, rising,
glowing with undignified light,

behind the veil of life,
all is found,

iridescent

—noticed, discovered
by the light,
in every corner and crevice.

This is the awakening,
this is the returning.

Here, the wind is caressing my cheek,
reminding me it's safe,
to feel — feel everything.
would i embrace it all?
Suffer well without shields.

Feasting on acceptance,
until my belly is a heap of wheat
encircled with lilies.

Abandonly soft,
Clay on a Potter's wheel

Oh lord,
turn me
into a city

"We don't let go into trust, until we've exhausted our egos."
—Rob Lehman

Burning House

August 27, 2021
Lake Eufaula, Oklahoma
10:08 p.m.

I had a dream about a burning house:
you were stuck inside,
I couldn't get you out.

I was all alone,
I yelled for you to run and flee,
but you never heard me,
the roar of the flames too loud.

I grieved, grasping the open door
as I felt your screams in the depths of me.

You wanted me to come in,
to lay beside you, helpless,
pull you close and suffocate—
the two of us engulfed in smoke.

It was the only way
you learned how to be close.

This dream has reoccurred constantly,
and now I'm sleepwalking while I'm awake.

Ruminating on if you'll ever choose
to get out of that damn burning house.

It's been over 20 years that I've been out here,
searching for you in the ruins, all alone.

I know the smoke's deep in your lungs,
you don't think you have the strength
to carry on.

Carry on.

Still, I know there's no way
for me to ever help you escape.

So here's where I have to forgive
what's broken and
what will continue to break,
like the frame of that burning house
that's held and still holds you.

You'll never know just how much
it broke me down,

just how much

I pounded my fists to the ground.

You truly cannot understand loss,
only feel it, feel all its merciless flames.

But I promise, though I cannot come in,
I'll stay outside this door,
begging for you to step out
into the light and embrace the wind.

here I'll forgive
here I'll pray
here I'll hope
here I'll stay

Dependency

August 31, 2022
Lake Eufaula, Oklahoma
11:00 p.m.

There's warm water to my chest,
as I'm praying to God for help.

The clouds are outside inventing themselves,
change is coming,
the wind is picking up,
do you feel it?

In the waiting room of the unknown,
may we not be found flipping coins,
simply saying "tails or heads?"

The voice of God
doesn't work like that;
we're so much more free.

So when it's all up in the air—
ask yourself, what's keeping you here?

A legalistic man is flipping a black and white coin into a well he
didn't dig and is calling it reverence.

A hardened heart is leaning a questioning ear against a wall.
At least they're leaning.
A curious adolescent has a Styrofoam cup
on a string, giddy, just around the corner,
while a son's head rests
against his mother's chest,
listening to her heartbeat.

His voice is not formed from thin air.
It forms the space we breathe.

And we are formed by
what we are believing
about the One who is listening.

Jesus, come.
Further heal trust in me,
to discern rightly.
the sound of your voice.

These creases
from smiling,
around my eyes
—may they deepen,
like the banks of the Red Sea parting.

May they remind me of the faithfulness of your leading,

renewing my mind's ability to believe,
to hear beyond my limited perceiving,
in the hallways of waiting.

Jesus, teach me dependency.

"Show me yourself, and I'll swim to you."
—Mark Nepo

You're in My Veins

August 26, 2020
Lake Eufaula, Oklahoma
12:54 a.m.

If English is a language,
then so is silence in our family.

Everything heard but nothing said,
yet I've felt your screams for years.

They say blood is thicker than water,
though it's heavier to hold,
and hell to wade through.

But you're in my veins,
I'll continually, always choose you.

Let the Veil Be Torn

September 6, 2022
Dallas, Texas
10:33 a.m.

The goal is to live at the thin place,
where the veil is completely torn,
where all of you is at the surface,
like waves upon the ocean—
unrestrained, consistently breaking,
fully present,
holding nothing back—
and you live a thousand years,
not in succession, but
in every breath.

This doorway is always near;
to be joyfully overwhelmed
by the fabric of existence
in which everything,
even pain,
carves out a river
that widens our ability to hold
truth, joy and beauty.

This risk, to step into the secrets; hidden
in the open waters of our busy lives

a very quiet and present threshold
that reminds us,
there truly is *nothing between us.*

Nothing between the forests and our teeth,
between the sands and our eyes,
between the oceans and our hearts,
between the inevitable sufferings and splendors,
between the unseen and unheard
—everything living affecting everything else.

We are not alone.
For all of life's comforts and fears,
we are never alone.

Let the veil be torn.

*Some stanzas were lifted, paraphrased, and rearranged from Mark Nepo's book, *The Exquisite Risk.*

An Ode to the Swing

September 21, 2022
Redding, California
1:19 p.m.

When I got too old for my own good,
when the clouds stood hovering
in the undercurrent of heartbreak,
you reminded me:

how to let time stand still,
reversing the whirlpool in my mind;
how to absorb the light—whole—
feel my chest crack open and breathe,
running in an open space filled with memories,

    where courage looked like honest tears,
      streaming under the setting sun of Redding;

of the kid inside of me, a fire that must burn,
passionately screaming, free-spirited,
unconfined to dream, and fully worthy.

You paced yourself
to the rhythm of my heartbeat
for hours, as God wrapped His naked body
around my vulnerability

—as long as I needed, you stayed with me,
grounded by the motion,
the push and pull of your gravity,
as His scarred hands caressed
my flushed, blood-red cheeks.

Thank you, you held space for me
—an ode to the swing,
the swing that consoled me.

Never Separate

A prayer

Penetrate my heart and let it bleed,
consume ever fiber of my being.

Help me
to let love cost me.

Lead me through the wound in your side—
keep me warm under the cross of Calvary,
your blood becoming my lens,
continually pouring over my eyes.

Help me to drink
the wine of your spirit
—the only thing that sobers me.

Yeshua, please sober me.

I completely yield
all of me.

Bind us together on that tree,
sharing scars in both of our hands and feet,
together, in union,
rising delivered, ascending.

Forever reveal this deeper to me,
the revelation of the cross,
just how much your flesh was the veil torn in two,
the cleft in the Rock, where I now hide in you.

Show me just how
inseparable, irrevocable, incorruptible your love is,
like red dye mixing with blue.

Jesus, I need you, to love you.
And I do,
I love you. I love you. I love you.

Percolate me
with the revelation of our union,
this living hope, this undying Truth.

We are
never separate,
your blood flowing in mine.

How it really does take two
to make a thing go right.

Celestial

September 23, 2022
Malibu, California
9:02 p.m.

"I was sitting on the beach,
minding my own business, and
I just got demolished by the tide
—now all of me is soaked."
// a text message sent at 8:43 p.m.

Now there's a group of girls
scream-singing Whitney
behind me, and very rightly so.

Because don't we all
just want to dance with somebody,
somebody who loves us?

Experience a rush,
a feeling like the tide
that wakes you up
when you're run dry.

"I don't know where I'm going,
to be honest,"

says one of the girls,
as they've now walked
to where I'm lying,
soaked in the sand
that's molding to my body.

Her friends respond to her honesty,
they help lead her.

Now I'm watching a couple race in the sand;
I think to myself,
I'm going to miss this.

They tumbled in front of me,
giggling, now they're wrestling,
like us all.

But they're doing it together
—so they're laughing

and gasping as they come closer,
now able to see me in the dark,

"Oh! There are people here!"

I laugh back and say,
"Yeah, I'm right here."

Isn't the Father like that,
always near,
able to be seen in the dark,
if only you simply choose to draw near?

For even in the night,
the moonlight
is light.

Here, I feel the Milky Way
smiling above me

       and so am I.

Studying the world,
letting it unfold me
at my page's edge,
soaked in the sand,
overtaken
by the power of the ocean
without choice or strife.

Under the shadow
of the night light,
all feels celestial,
reverent, and right.

Water in the Desert

September 25, 2022
Joshua Tree, California
12:11 p.m.

You'll always have more
—if you're generous,
like the water rushing
through the cracks
of the boulders beside
me, consistently overflowing,
eroding, softening the hardened places
in a desert, a desert
with miraculous, bountiful beauty.

It's not to be avoided, whatever
one means by a dry season.

The cross struck the Rock,
now all that's dry has become
space to be filled with an oasis
that is ever overflowing.

If ever and when you feel distant,
like true north,
always return to honesty.

Behind every hard shell,
there's an abundance
of oxygen, of presence,
of giving.

There truly is water in the rocks
of the desert. I'm next to them.

To experience burnout—the drought of the shallow end—
is a kind of mercy, man's striving;
what kindness, to allow you to come to the end of yourself.

His arms are wide open,
enter in.

Nothing makes sense outside of Him,
we are made to lose ourselves fully to holy communion.

Hear the sound of warm rushing waters clear away all confusion,
His voice increasing in volume.
His voice,
the abundance that meets our every need.

By the Spirit, find strength to remain soft,
on your knees.

Do not rely on self,
there is no more reason
to ever go without

—*our daily bread.*

The Kitchen Floor

September 25, 2022
Joshua Tree, California
7:19 p.m.

My knees are on the cold tile floor,
leaning over you with tears, saying
"Just look at my eyes."

You didn't want to live anymore,
together we held your hand
—it wasn't the first time
a life was saved on the kitchen floor.

Your hair sprawled against the ground,
we stayed low with you, lying next to you,
as long as it took, never leaving,
until your exhausted eyes could find ours
in that blue dilapidated house—
that house that still holds our laughs,
an album of our sounds—
you opened your bloodshot eyes
in magnificent and radiant courage,
you were found

—all we ever need is eye contact.

To know you can't put
hope to death, even
if hope deferred
makes you want to.

That hope is forever undying
and always able to be found,
not just a feeling but a presence
all around,
held in each other's eyes,
in the deepest of deserts,
at twilight, I promise this,
here and now.

Now you're living, glowing,
full of wonder, so beautiful,
so alive.
I hear your laugh
in my backseat
as I'm driving cross country—
I didn't expect to hear you here,
but I love you; what we shared that night
marked me.

I'm still processing when my knees hit the ground in grief,
alone on the phone with my mother,
in the middle of the Isla Vista streets.

Her voice shaking, "He took his own life."

He was like an uncle to me.

I had to swallow all the air I had left
to face the days ahead, to avoid
constantly wanting to fall to the ground
and somehow find him there,
still breathing.

It's weird how gravity
is ripped out like a rug from underneath
when we need it most.

I guess sometimes you have to get so low,
face in the dirt, to find hope.

Like the pain of looking at the sun directly,
I've stared at this fully,
but that doesn't mean it still hasn't left me seeing blurry.

Though I'm so unafraid of death now,
my windows are rolled all the way down
—here, I am laughing.

Remember the to-go coffee I gave you,
where my ink was spilled out on the sides?

You just lost someone you loved,
someone dear and nothing made sense,
all was suspended and disoriented.

I write to you all because of this,
to those I've seen overcome, my hand in theirs,
and to those I've lost to suicide that I wish could read this,
with everything in me:

I implore you to choose life,
and know that Hope is a Person,
who is very real.

Hope is in the very air we breathe,
inside your lungs,
forever tangibly surrounding.
I've seen His eyes.
He has delivered all of me.

Draw near, *take courage*
open your eyes,
reach out your hand,
be found.

Love is here.
Love is *right here.*

This is truer than life itself,
hope will always remain
and prevail.

Consider the Silence

September 25, 2022
Joshua Tree, California
9:25 p.m.

This night, the stars are swimming above me
while the gentleness of the breeze
feels like God Himself,
a mercy, soothing as warm honey.

Silence and solitude befriend me
here among the cacti;
everything is strikingly holy.

Again, I find it true,
compartmentalization only exists in the mind,
though how much do we avoid reality, the reality

       that all things are integrated?

And for what?
To shove aside what we don't want to face?
Our full selves in a mirror,
the pain we don't know how to grapple with,
the lie that somehow understanding
would heal the wounds, these wounds
we were never meant to deal with.
Whatever you're thinking of, that's it

—and ignore it all? A future boomerang.

And if it all doesn't have to make sense—

then what?

Yielded.
Your presence on a pillow next to mine,
when I can't sleep at night.
Your body, carved into mine at the rib.

Daily *with us* in the middle of it all,
where the frayed parts are most thin,
in the contrasts between the black and white,
pain and joy,
the day and night.

For isn't it true that the color black
absorbs the rainbow?

Isn't it true that the night shines bright as the day?
Isn't it true that the depths of joy can't be discovered without
the purifying fire of pain?
Pain, which is never our enemy.

A sacred mundanity,
a holy hush,
this gift of existence, *it is enough.*

And more than anything—

       consider the silence,

for it does not judge the night.

Listen to its reverent humility,
can you feel it making you aware
of the mirages of your fear?
Suddenly, how memories surface,
as it begins teaching you how to trust,
to behold, to embrace, to remember
inside its eviscerating mirror.

How it leans itself kindly toward you,
inviting you to pour out your disappointment,
emotions, dreams which have been suppressed.

A blanket, it covers,
it woos, hemming you into connection.

Like the stars that watch over you,
that you hardly stop for long enough
to gaze—

to gaze upward,
to gaze inward,
to gaze at all
would be enough.

Consider the silence,

how it raises the volume in your chest.

Suddenly you become aware of your breath,
all the strife begins to slow down,
repressed tears begin to stream down your cheeks;
a gift,
showing you what truly matters,

and how much you care.

You whisper out loud without realizing, "*It's just about being a good friend.*"

Consider the silence,

you've now stepped outside of yourself
—shedding the blindfolds of the ego—
the air is thin, the air is clear,
fault is not weakness, *lack of ownership is;*
there is so much space here.

Consider the silence,

so much to repent of,
to forgive,
to lament,
to give,
to honor,
(for heaven's sake, love your parents!)
to now, *oh, now to understand!*

Here in the letting go, it's all beginning to make sense!

Consider the silence,

how God is found within,
inviting us home again.

Feel the release,
the breath of salvation.

Consider the silence,
always speaking—revealing,
God's smile,
forever accepting.

How it leads you to a safe open field,
soft and still among the lilies.

Preeminence

September 26, 2022
Grand Canyon, Arizona
6:44 p.m.

Sometimes there really are no words,
sometimes your legs just tremble,
and you feel your heart swell, then race.

Sometimes you just can't stop staring;
take notice of those moments—those who
take your breath away.

See, it's majesty
that will be preeminent and permeate,
washing all that can be shaken away.

Feel the rush of chills clothe your flesh,
let the rattling in your bones
draw you to your knees, to see clearly again.

You are a kid, your stomach swims
with lightning bugs caught in an alabaster jar,
warm tears roll down your face.

As you stand through a sunroof,
in the rolling hills of Northern Ireland,

as you gaze on the face of someone you love,
taking them in, simply never wanting to look away.

As the windows are rolled down all the way,
always, just so you can feel the fullness of it all
in the desert, listening to Angels & Airwaves,
as you watch the sunset pour itself out,
in billowing splendor over the Grand Canyon.

Joy

—is this near, always.

It is the most vulnerable emotion;
what bravery to feel the world inside out—

remain there, let it enfold you.

Because here, love is perfected.
Here, fear cannot remain.

This Body

July 31, 2021
Redding, California
3:06 p.m.

Unearth it all,
flood me with light
so I can see everything.
I don't care if it makes me scream;
I ache to know myself fully—

my flesh, this blood and water
formed from the ground I stand upon,

this body, holy
this body, altogether lovely
this body, worthy
this body, forgotten
looked past, made invisible

this body, forgiving for when my eyes
were avoiding, piercing, unaccepting,
shut down to its feelings.

Numbness is not just in relation to the heart,
it's when a woman's survival, apathy, begrudging
become the opposite of love from the start—

disassociated to every atom woven intricately,
to the skin that holds me,
fractured by the constant lack of safety,
this measuring stick against me.

Though, how kind,
so loving, so trustworthy,
to heal even when it's cut
with eyes by man, by self, or thoughts unseen,
unacknowledged, ignored femininity.

Oh, but how you are a direct reflection
of the glory of divinity,
like the moon,
and how I murdered you in fear of fragility,
how wrong I was—I'm sorry.

This air about me,
strength and divine delicacy,
not like the sand that can be moved,
but like water,
soft enough to run your hands through,
yet strong enough to hold a ship,
Womanhood.

My sexuality,
I'm sorry I suffocated you.

I heard it wasn't safe,
that it was to be controlled,
if I let you past the gates.

Body, I love you, always have,
even when I didn't know how,
and now I'll choose you,
eyes accepting of every fiber of you,
naked, unashamed, unburied,
fully in touch with all that forms me,
attuned with all of Who formed
this wonderful body.

The pleasures of heaven you carry,
the pains of hell you've felt—
the first, I graft into and increase,
the latter, ever redeemed.

Oh, to be a woman,
to mother, birth, and provide life,
from the same thing
that makes a man surrender,
breast to mouth,
how stunningly formidable, wildly reverent,
altogether lovely, worthy of acceptance—
this body.

Angry
A remembrance

Baylor University
Waco, Texas

"Micaela, punch me."

I'm alone in my closet, so angry,
resistant in feeling on my knees.

"Punch me."

Jesus leans near, close to my face,
whispering.

"Punch me."

"No."

"Punch me."

"Damnit, no."

"Micaela, punch me."

Jesus is now crying, His hands on my face, trying to lift my chin.
My teeth are gritted, fierce, my hands white-knuckled. Anger.

"Love, punch me."

"Jesus, no. Why would you even ask this of me right now?"

"My love, punch me."

I break.

> Beating a cardboard box that sits in front of me, holding
> picture frames of memories.
> His chest, my fists are pounding.

The dam of grief suddenly breaking in my soul.
I am weak, on the floor. Weeping.

I am soft again, a river flowing. I am yielded against Him, given
into His strength.

He holds me so tight against His body. Not letting go. I can feel
His heartbeat,
fast, in tune with mine.

> *"Micaela, I had to have you punch me so you
> would stop punching yourself.*

All the loss isn't your fault.
I know how much they meant.
Stay near. Stay here.
Let me take it all on,
punch me everywhere it hurts."

Your Eyes

A prayer

There is no anger in your eyes
—Holy Spirit, please help there be none in mine.

Beyond Memory

October 9, 2022
Dallas, Texas
10:49 a.m.

There's water in the palm of your hands,
your eyes beholding its mirroring.

Though, what becomes of the memories?

The water reflected back at you
when you let it go
in loss, will you lose them too?

In this fragile state,
you choose to open your hands,
as the water bleeds
over your fingers,
the blur is clearing,
and an open meadow
in a forest is singing,
resuscitating the gift of hope

that is now drenched
in a connected reality
—beyond memory,
anchored deep,
rising forward

inside a dream

an assurance of goodness,
in our future
—we're smiling.

Gethsemane

November 15, 2022
Dallas, Texas

My feet tread holy ground,
I'm barefoot, the soles of my feet against the soft grass,
In the Garden of Gethsemane.
Oh, I can hear Him now, in anguish,
My heart lurching, leaping, burning,
He is bent over weeping in front of me,
Clothed in my humanity,
Deep overwhelming sorrow,
He is sweating blood from His forehead,
His hands are white at the knuckles,
From gripping,
He is carrying all of me.

My hands are now reaching forward toward Him,
I'm aching! My friend, my love!
I wrap my arms around His chest from behind,
To comfort Him as I break internally at a depth
I cannot begin to describe,
Bursting in guttural sobs with Him,
He gasps, shuddering at my touch,
Heaving, He can barely breathe.

I tighten my grip around Him,

"Father, take this cup from me!"
My cheek now against His beard,
Pressed fully against Him,
Our tears entwining,
Cradling the One who formed me,
Our breath heavy, in shared pain,
Our chests rising and falling in unison,
He turns His face around,
Now His bloodshot eyes look into mine,
He gasps again in relief to see me,
He buries His face into my neck,
As I hold Him, we're both weak with love.
Vulnerably, I whisper, my voice cracking through tears,
"You won me, my love. You get all of me.
I'm here. Thank you, oh thank you, Jesus!
I'm with you forever now. It's worth it."

We're laughing and weeping at the same time.
Completely won by the other.

To Be Human

The prayer room
Dallas, Texas
May 23, 2023
2:25 p.m.

You never ignore the pain.
You never shy away.

In you, there is no shame.
You stay present.

You break all the rules.
You are the rules.

You ask all the best questions.
You rest inside tension.

You teach me what it is,
to be human.

A deep breath, an interlude:

"The maturity I thought I would find in powering through came in eye contact and telling the truth—the bravery was being messy without agenda. The breakthrough isn't that I'm out of anything—it's that I'm not alone in it. I'm not using breakthrough as the end of a chapter or an exhale that something has ended. Just that truth is truth and with it comes gratitude. Cutting through the over-serious nature of the shame of not knowing and joining the journey of my own sanctification. My eyes opening to the awe of access to the Creator in the tiny rituals of the day; waiting in the pouring of the coffee and insistence on the use of china cups and glassware. He is holy. I wanted solutions and strategies. Vision and relief. Instead I got dropped into my own pain where I was awake to everything I was afraid of. I thought I could get saved out of being myself but being saved from yourself just drops you into more authenticity."

—Allie Elmore

To My Future Husband

January 7, 2022
Whiskeytown, California
2:34 p.m.

I desire a tale of safety and peaceful mornings,
where the mundane becomes on fire
and we get to unravel into each other,
extraordinarily messy and full of whimsy,
like a child finger-painting onto a canvas
or a warm afternoon of gentle summer rain—

       and it's always just to be with you,
to discover your eyes that hold you
    (all of you)
       every aspect unhindered, unhidden
    (protected)
may we be home, together

Wheat

Years ago, still present
Mustang, Oklahoma
4:16 p.m.

You whispered,
"My love, I am your home."
I am lying
among endless
harps of golden wheat,
the Oklahoma sun
burning,
the wind,
like my mind,
a symphony.

I surrender my hands to the weight
of gravity, everything that pulls me,

my hands
are soaked with my tears.

My voice is tired,
from shouting.
My breath, heavy.

I am hidden.

I am held among the shafts of wheat,
the light melting, like honey
through the stalks, gently beckoning,
"Be still."

I ran here—sprinting,
too good at enduring

running,
                    running,

running,

                    running

away from all, all
that hurt,
and what hurt?
Everything,
                    unseen.

I am 15.

Warm tears run down my blood-red cheeks,
my messy golden-brown hair is strewn against
the golden blanket of the earth,
fighting for grounding.

I am red.

Like the dirt that raised me,
like blood spilled out.

Your eyes were emerald green.

Your eyes.
This was the first time I saw them,
kinder than anything I've ever seen,
so much, I couldn't even breathe.

You had warm tears running down
your blood-red cheeks,
sharing the pain in me.

Your welcoming, vastly amber-green
tender eyes wouldn't leave mine, piercing
all of me.

In that wide-open wheat field,
that held no fences,
you swallowed all the space in between—

and again, I am a little
6-year-old girl.

Wildly curious, wide-eyed
fierce-yet-ever-so-innocently-soft
honestly tender
raw-bushy-pony-tailed
T-shirt-too-big girl
who cried when she saw her breath
in the cold air and was still
and knew with every fiber of her being,
you were God.

You are God
and I am loved.

Never alone.

Whispering Alabaster

July 15, 2021
Redding, California
2:02 p.m.

how i wanted to be that sky
that holds every shooting star
where the moon opens a door to the more
—beyond

    it's not far.

tell me it wasn't a waste. the search for an oasis in a sun-beaten
valley. this hunger. this thirst. thirst is to give the heart what it
longs for. the tongue what it calls out for in every hidden place.

vain.

my vein thumping against your skin, my heartbeat like a
sunflower, growing toward the heart in your chest

within.

    thirst is what holds us here.

sunrise: a lasso of magenta honey shepherding life back to
awakening.

The morning dew pushing back the shadows like a rush of blood to the head.

How utterly sobering is the faithfulness of mercy.

birds chirping, do you hear them? Do they notice me? the way i notice them. do eyes see past the mirror within. do eyes truly see at all past their own lens?

where's light, that it would fall through the bedroom window of our worlds? inviting you. inviting me. to climb out of our living rooms of self-perception, deception.

disillusionment.

hands grasping for each other. for themselves really, reaching for origin—longing for belonging.
gnawing on bones—striving.

this throne inside me!
dismantle it.
this crown!
rip it down.

humility is an ocean where i'll happily drown.

and have you ever tried to scream
but your head was underwater

talking to anyone who would listen
though they won't be silent enough

present enough, to hear
the whispers coming off the walls

it goes on even farther.

—the voice of your own heart.

look, everyone is in love with their own tongue

it's where we fall.

not like autumn
—like inevitable pain.

damnit, make sense of it and control yourself, said the
seriousness of shame.

say surrender!

but it's hard! *hard to be soft.*

say you'll stay when i bleed. say you'll open up your skin and let
me take shelter within.

drowning in your arms,

stay.

You starting where i end.
Your sea becoming my land.

at the shoreline of the soul
whispering alabaster, again and again.

i found myself in a broken mirror,
searching like we all do
for a reflection that would tell me the whole truth,
teach me how to retrace these steps,
to what feelings,
what innocence, has left. no longer making sense.

buried in itself.

grown over, grow inward to grow out
—of these wounds like that sunflower
reaching for yours inside your own chest.

these wounds i healed—performed!
these wounds, i thought were healed.

i kept trying to catch their eyes
but they look beyond me
back at themselves

i don't want to be like them
lost inside the cocoon of self,
—*the selfishness of never changing*

i want to fully see, with extraordinary clarity
so here i am learning, how to
swallow the self whole compassionately
and choke on what's limiting,
then die.

finally to awake,
like a metamorphosed white butterfly
to then see

                    the full spectrum of light.

Have you ever purposely colored outside the lines?

we're all open fields with no fences

order isn't absent of messiness, i would do anything for you, would you be yourself

that's just mentos inside a closed

off coke bottle a.k.a. perfectionism

what if beauty is everywhere, remember to whisper thank you

don't get overwhelmed, keep looking

333 you could find a four leaf clover

you saw it too growth is divine easy tiger! red rover,

did it move you? red rover

what is have you ever colored outside of the lines on purpose? I prefer to not

walk on the sidewalk

the sky is only blue liberation there's so much

i did, they weren't pleased. because of the reflection of light! more room!

I understand

reformation have you allowed yourself to swim,

like this-try the butterfly stroke, honesty is nobility,

first it'll feel like you can't see your own hand in the dark :) choose bravery,

why are you holding back? what are all we why does everything have to be so damn tidy? over and over,

so afraid of? daily

We know nothing! What a gift! let's spill wine on ourselves,

you be blue let's get messy i love you

i'll be red self-portrait: why are my parents in the mirror?

lean into I love

consider the lilies what offends your mind, you

let them teach you discover the spectrum the 90's <3 cross lateral thinking

between black and white I love you

let go of timidity intermission - the flowers you gave me are now petals floating here I am, with no fig leaves

upstream whispering secrets to me up up up an unbridled wild horse

i loved you

inside my dreams means in in in

i'm okay unless

when you close your eyes with being wrong...are you? we what are you?

at night, do you think of me? we've got nothing to lose

but dignity, step into mystery

sounds really freeing perspective is a prism, tic-tac toe!

a stream of consciousness: let light in and see what happens have some

I'm having fun, (it should be explained that a "fence" would be the denial and suppression fun!

wanna join me? of expression, of emotion, of life, of what's real)

Jesus is the door you're looking for

and again, we're inside c'mon, let's get real honest

cardboard boxes that are spaceships! the entryway is where the exit signs are,

p.s. the password is, "let go"

no more where's waldo? shame is oh so serious

hide and seek tell me, how has your ego

stay soft at all costs YIELD boundless & served you

unconfined lets just dance a lil',

innocent like fresh snow in the morning shall we...wanna tango?

"Would we become water,
and let grief rinse the depths of us,
so to reflect as much light as we can?"
—Mark Nepo

All Is Sober

November 21, 2022
Mustang, Oklahoma
12:31 a.m.

Everything has slowed down,
nothing matters, yet everything does.

Your hand on my hand,
your heart, beating.

Your eyes, speaking,
your life in front of me.

Pain, yours,
now held in my arms
when you are
too weary.

When we are faced
head on with death
—*suddenly*,
like slipping
into an ocean of ice—

  all is sober.

My skin
extends
outwardly,
for anything,
yet understanding
cannot clothe me.

Only feeling,
everything.

Your hand,
reaching
near,

> *here,*
> *with you*

as long as time permits me,
is all that matters.

Turn Me into a Lily

November 29, 2022
Tonbridge, UK
12:42 p.m.

If I break, would you let me in?
Be quiet and stay with me if I shatter?

I'm asking
—would you help me,

                    put these fists down?

I'm lying against the endless mysterious sky,
unafraid of all I do not know,
looking past the shadows toward the sun,
with my emerald, hazel eyes
—I am swelling,
in the spill of light.

This boundlessness
—the vast liberation of truth—
is where I choose to remain,
until the day breathes,
and the shadows flee.

Here, the wind is caressing my cheek,

reminding me it's safe
to feel—feel everything.

Would I embrace it all?
Suffer well without shields,
swallowing acceptance,
until my belly is a heap of wheat
encircled with lilies.

Abandonedly soft,
clay on a potter's wheel.

Oh God, shatter all defensiveness,
the ego's false pretensions and
all its rigid confinements.

Turn me into a flower,
like you,
a lily
of the valley.

Humble, sensitive to the wind,
malleable,
reliant on the light
—blooming,
with no end.

Not just yearning
for the reflection
that I want more than the truth.

The pressure,
the hope,
the dream,
the want,
I could never get to,
alone.

Because when its smoke is gone,
on the other side it's always just been you.

Me, in love,
you, holding all of my pieces,
innocent and altogether beautiful,
a child filled with wonder
—peering through the kaleidoscope of your love,
home in your comforting arms,
held in the gravity of your reality.

No more striving to be enough
—no more defending,
only fully given in, losing myself
to being swaddled, hidden within your being.

Unguarded and honest,
altogether lovely.

Like a flower,
that cannot silence its innate beauty.

Oh God, turn me into a lily.

Space for You

December 5, 2022
Southfields, London
1:58 p.m.

I remember when I saw you repent,
tears streaming down your face,
vulnerable in your living room;
it moved every part of me.

Look at me, I love you,
there's an open field,
so much unending space for you.

In all your pain,
in all your messiness,
in all your joy,
there is space for you.

You have my friendship;
loyal, I'll draw near,
I'll stay right here,
with you.

Linger

December 1, 2022
65mm Coffee
Tonbridge, UK
1:01 p.m.

Not in a hurry,
been here for hours,
my lips quiver
as your presence
overwhelms me.
I feel you from head to toe,
huddled in this corner alone,
but not lonely,
in this quaint coffee shop,
by a river in England.

My soul gasps,
tasting the wine
of your relentless love—
you're so alive,
my skin rises to attest to
such a glorious truth.

What unending beauty,
that awakens every fiber of my being!

Stay right here,
I just want to stay right here,
sweetly lingering.

Present, intentional,
oh, just to be with you, always.

My prayer, Jesus,
is that you would feel safe in the garden of my chest,
my most cherished friend, that in me, you would find a home to
rest.

May I be found leaning on my Beloved,
coming for nothing you can give,
but to simply enjoy the pure delight of communion,
our sweet sweet friendship.

The intoxicating rise and fall of your breath,
with my head on the skin of your chest, always.

Lover, *let's linger.*

These Are the Whispers

December 4, 2022
London, UK
12:41 p.m.

I am a root
of an oak tree,
planted by a vast
unending ocean

I am light, bleeding
through the cracks,
refracting through a prism

I am a firefly,
dancing in the night

I am a hand, reaching
gliding through water

I am a memory, swelling
in the palm of your hand

These are the whispers,
tearing down my walls,
oxygen expanding my lungs

I am smiling,
in this train station in central London

Grief Can Be Bright

January 7, 2023
Dallas, Texas
10:39 p.m.

Grief.

It is never to be void of the spirit of the illumination of God,
it is independency that is at war with discerning light.

Freedom is the choice;
to choose freedom or confines.

What are the boundary lines, where have they fallen?
Is it not in good places?

Are not the boundary lines, *Him?*
The outline of His very body revealing our inheritance,
our home to dwell in?

Unbelief is only but a self-inflicting separation
Leading to apathy resulting from self absorption,
survival and shields will only serve us so much,
living outside the boundary lines like being in space
without oxygen, before it stills our own blood entirely,
making us numb.

*This poem is deeply inspired from a sermon by Melissa Helser; the first two lines are direct qoutes from her.

The Fear of the Lord keeps us warm,
the utter conviction that He is safe,
remaining in Him,
in the deepest of valleys,
in the most confusing paths of pain.

Staying grounded in contact with reality,
is what it means to fight for love,
gritty and undone,
sitting within the tension,
when all feels against us.

He never turns His back.

Go back to where it hurts the most,
honest honest honest
until the dam is broken,
the blinds completely opened,
where then,
all slackens,
tethered in Him—our inheritance.

Eroding

November 13, 2022
Dallas, Texas
12:03 p.m.

Pride is the bedrock of all sin.

Humility is the highest goal.

Transcend the selfishness of the ego.

What we judge, we cannot understand.

What we cannot understand, we divide ourselves from.

Where we divide ourselves, we cannot be touched.

Where we cannot be touched, we are aching.

This loneliness is only cured by contact with reality;

Oh, how

we take ourselves way too seriously!

For where there is conflict,

there is simply no understanding.

Where there is defensiveness,

there is a lack of awareness.

But it hurts more to stay the same

than to yield, grow, and change.

The more revelation we receive,

the higher the responsibility.

Come up here,

your spirit doesn't need healing,

it needs to come alive.

The mind is not the spirit but the spirit flows through the mind,

so expand, un-restrict, let down the walls of fear,

experience the depths of the river of life.

The spirit leading, rushing, eroding,

ever overflowing.

How wonderful it is to be awake!

To ever grow,
to truly be alive.

Liminal Space

February 7, 2023
Dallas, Texas
10:47 a.m.

Like an emerald gem
being upheaved from the earth,
jagged and frayed at the edges,
His hand reaches, not to prune,
but to refine
all that's blocking out the light

So I'll sit soberly,
in this liminal space
tonight,
weakly full of strength,
breathing in tune,
rising and falling,
over and over again,
dependent like a rib to His side

Ache

March 16, 2023
Dallas, Texas
2:45 p.m.

You didn't notice,
but I watched you the other day,
the silhouette of your body dancing.

Tears welled up in my soul,
I ached for your life.

You were so beautiful,
miraculously being.

Wish Upon a Dandelion

March 26, 2023
Dallas, Texas
4:40 p.m.

We're together.

My head resting on the skin of your chest,
I am vulnerable.

You pull my hair back behind my ear
and whisper
"You are my wish upon a dandelion."

As the light of your face
baptizes me again and again
—ecstatic intimacy.

I am the moon,
you are my gravity,
shining in the reflection,
of your countenance.

The oil of your joy,
filling every crevice in my heart
with undying strength.

Jesus, my Delight, my Love,
let me adorn you with the
poured-out fragrance of my adoration.

Let me handpick
all the flowers!

Uproot all the beauty
in the world!

Just for you.

This is all for you.

I am your bride,
fully given,
there is no other
for me.

You too
are my wish upon a dandelion.

Safe

February 7, 2023
Dallas, Texas
10:38 p.m.

Soft and delicate,
like white tissue paper,
unwrapped and opened from a gift.

I keep daydreaming

of simply laying my head on your shoulder.

Where there is no passivity,
your presence asserting itself,
with your arms around me.

Me, a flower—that lily,
walls down, safe,
no longer striving;
you, my stem,
upholding me.

I need
the vitalness of
your masculinity.

Mom & Dad

May 6, 2023
Dallas, Texas
1:53 p.m.

Mom, I love you.

Do you remember when you
taught me how to draw a lily?

My little legs were dangled over your
bathroom counter, I was looking at myself in the mirror.

With a smile, you had a pen and some torn-out paper.

You had no idea,
how much that moment would mean to me.

It was the tiniest glimpse,
I doubt you even remember it,
but I doodled it on paper, constantly.

Now it's tattooed on my arm with meaning unending.

Mom, you are the most perseverant and compassionate.

A depth of treasure, full of sacrificial love and care.

Only you know how much it all has cost you,
but, Mom, *I see you*—fully worthy, incredibly beautiful.

...

Dad, this is for you.

I've never known someone more faithful, so loyal and true.

You remain noble, within the fire, through and through.

Remember the telescope you got me that one Christmas?

The one I would stand outside with.

Under the blanket of the stars for hours, staring at the moon.

The moon, your provision allowed me to believe, I could get to.

Dad, thank you.

Forever, I love you.

Kindred

April 11, 2023
Noble Coyote Roasters
1:29 p.m.

There's a freckle on your left hand,
below your index,
to the left of your thumb.

I was always
paying attention

—to your eyes—

to all of you,
a vast unending ocean.

Like the one we walked into
—where you led me,
submerging hand in hand in my dream.

That was years ago,
since, you've exhumed and eviscerated
the depths of me—unnoticing,
until all is disorienting.

My indelible kindred friend,
I'll never fall in love for the first time again.

And like a dying seed,
fallen to the ground,
only to be buried,
here I lay down the shovel entirely.

Where I've been *aching*,
for it all to make sense
—no longer in denial and resistance,
making contact with all that's been true,
taking root to bloom anew.

We're nearly Earth already.

Passenger Seat

March 26, 2023
Dallas, Texas
12:12 a.m.

He came to me.
The child beneath.

His tears wiped mud off my eyes,
the scars in His hands,
my alibi

—defense,
no longer in me.

There's an orange crayon,
the color of the sunrise in my left hand,
and I'm connecting the dots,

> *an only child in the passenger seat,*
> *playing M.A.S.H—pining for mirroring.*
>
> *reaching,*
> *for someone to share this with.*
>
> *how could you not blame me?*

I'm looking out into the open fields,
while the car is leaving.

Hoping to be like them,
open and known with no boundary.

Though I was never pursued,
through all my own split screens,
like how your back is now turned to me,
wearing an old patterned fleece,
avoiding.

> *and have you found an isolated room so quiet*
> *all the walls turned into mirrors?*

this room, where I've been spinning
—like water draining—
a brave little girl, hoping
to make sense of it, *trying*
to just face this honestly

> *God how I need honesty*

But there are no windows in here.

the deafening silence echoed in me,
each time you would draw near then leave,

stockholmsvy—an unknowing reenacting,

made a lover out of abandoning

that crayon, now blood red
still in my left hand
demanding to re-write the story
inside the walls, that just came closer and closer
suppressing, inside this hide and seek

never confessed this till now—

in this landscape of longing
loneliness was the dissonance.

where at times I have felt like this goodbye
will last for a lifetime,

peering through the voids in between my fingers,
waving still holding out for a—*"hello"*

I think I fell in love with letting go.

a way to keep the familiar longing close,
your hand—nearer than I've ever felt—
an intimacy yet to hold

like when my dad pushed me down

the hill in the backyard of the house I grew up in
just to learn how to ride a bike
getting up, after I fell over and over again

> *Tell me, was it all my fault?*
> *I never meant to fall.*

with scraped arms and knees,
stuck inside this Chinese handcuff,
—I've just never known how to give up,

> lacing up my running shoes,
> you and I—each other's passenger seat,
> intimate silent tears—unbuckling

> *I saw this coming*

> *But I swear just one more time*
> *around the block and*
> *I'll get the hang of this*

> just a kid with a red balloon,
> filled with passion to give,
> afraid to let go
> to the air, so mysterious and aloof

> the air that I've been grabbing at
> in this reach,

before you even came—yearning,

like we all do

just to fill all these gaps at the seams
tangled at the heartstrings,
where we're on a two-way street,
playing house,
pretending.

yet peering over the fence,
I can see your innocence,

a significant little boy that's pure,
wanting to do right and be good,
and you are
—good—very good,
picking roses off the bushes for others,
sensitive, cutting away the thorns
just so they can hold them,
dreaming wildly in wonder

—you didn't know.

is this what it means to relinquish control?
to let go of what I've always known.

Like the leaves that truly understand growth,

falling to the ground from their own branches
in tender spirals,

like a tornado,

just to exhale and become new again,

in those open fields
now cleared of debris
—awakening

It's never been just you,
I've been completely underwater too,
would you care enough,
to notice—the hooks?

Though in the riptide underneath,
I'm finding rescue does not come externally,

it is only ever embraced,
in the inner surrendering.

where I'm drenched in God's presence,
with warm tears on the floor whispering "thankfully"

Could forgiveness become our buoy?

I walked through the mirrors scared,

yet found myself behind the walls in the deeps.

now a grown woman,
who knows
from the inside out,
that I always was and always will be

worthy
—of the work.

of becoming.
of considering.
of choosing.
of learning.
of noticing.

> *of presence,*
> *aware and connected,*
> *on the shore of the heart,*
> *able to be fully affected,*
> *feeling the tender pull*
> *of the ocean's gentle salty breeze.*

Like what I felt, but didn't yet understand
when you first met me.

I'll stay on my knees,
I'll stay honest,
sobriety is relieving.

This is a repentance.

I'm sorry.

ps.

I can now ride my bike with no handle bars.
I think maybe it's in being willing to

                         f
              a
                  l
                       l

open-hearted, over and over again
—that we realize the ground
that holds us steady,
isn't really that far
where we discover,
safety to let go,
and *to let*—
entirely

pps.

I didn't have my editor touch this,
the most honest things are unpolished.

In a Different Light

While driving, headed to work.

March 13, 2023
Dallas, Texas
6:14 a.m.

Where there was salt in my lungs,
I see now how you were preserving me,
finally figured it out in the relinquishing.

Hindsight puts me on your shoulders,
a little girl in a yellow sundress,
protected on all sides by mercy.

High above the horizon
—seeing clearly,
in a different light.

Bleed for Me

A Reflection

December 5, 2022
Across the Atlantic Ocean
9:33 p.m.

Shaking everything that can be shaken,
rending the parts I try to hold together
tightly, even with a thin string,
becoming new to the shedding
of old things, old ways I thought were me
but were just shields I used to protect

how much I self-preserve,
hold these emotions,
hold you at a distance,
make you climb over walls,

how fear built all these fences

but worn like a rose, the petals are falling
against water that's warm,
His voice that's rushing, melting
every afraid, hardened part inside of me

Again and again, I feel Him say,
"*I need you to bleed for me*"

His words cutting my heart open,
where I'm no longer self-protecting,
now I'm spilled out, bursting,
like that light dripping through the window in my living room,
vulnerably illuminating all the dust in the air

I see it everywhere,
so sober to the places that have been hidden,
without the allowance of the light

I know now, I must do what costs me
especially, even if it cuts me
—the necessary pain

I'll believe and repent to the deepest of deep parts of me,
for unconditional love, for You, for others, for life, for awakening,

tenderly,

I'll bleed.

"I see all of creation; every good and colorful and brilliant thing, beauty itself, weaving and winding its way through iridescent feathers, surging falls, peaks in alpenglow, petals, leaves, fur, texture, color, light, breath. Every good and beautiful, holy and created thing. When I look into His eyes."

—Hailey Roberts

The Discernible Rainbow

March 14, 2023
The prayer room
1:20 p.m.

We could never look fully into His face
without falling dead in the overwhelming,
blinding light of His glory.

So He gave us a prism of His incarnation,
bending the light into an array of colors,
so we can discern the light from the inside.

This is the discernible rainbow,
where any gradient of greyscale
disintegrates into color as we awaken to the face of God,
in every aspect of ourselves and all of creation.

Such a potent spectrum of light!

Dancing, shimmering, consuming!

Wildly burning in our hearts,
just behind the veil,
sobering our minds.

Binding together every place of separation
through grace, by the fabric of abounding faith,
where we draw so *near, near, near,*
to truly see and touch effervescently,
the terrifyingly beautiful awakening light
—*that's in everything!*

There is no distance,
we are one,
held within
the prism of Him,
accepted, awakened,
our hearts' eyes fully enlightened.

This is union.

This is true love.
This is the gift of existence.
This is *iridescence.*

Iridescence

Our deepest calling
in this life is to continually root ourselves
in the unwavering reality of unconditional love,
that we could resist hardening,
resist fear, the attacking and withdrawing,
and keep our hearts courageously open,
tenderly ever-present, attentive
to the unending light of experience,
and so reflect the holiness of being,
unraveling the depths,
unearthing this pure gift of existence,
seeing vividly,
at every break,
in every ripple,
at every seam,
in every angle,
living fully **awake**,
iridescent

Jesus is alive.

He is a bloody man, who gave everything to be one with you.

Broken, we could never do enough to be made whole outside of Him.

Jesus is the answer and the door to all you long for, step into Him.

In all the questions, He has never left you.

He burns pure with emotions and thoughts, as we do.

I've run my hand over His scars in tears.

I've fallen into His eyes that burn with all-consuming fire.

I've pounded His chest with my fist, in need.

I've lain below the cross at Calvary,

while His cleansing blood has dripped all over me.

I've felt His hands hold my face,

His forehead up against mine,

so close I could feel His breathing.

I've rested against the cradle of His arms,

beside trees planted near still waters.

I've ridden on His white horse in victory.

I've comforted Him in pain at Gethsemane.

His voice is wine. His heart is honey.

He is truly alive.

He is my best friend, my love, my King, my everything.

His love is more real than the air you breathe.

Do not let pain and confusion of this world lie to you.

The Creator of the Universe is for you.

Meet this Man, be born again,

at His side, His wound that was sufficient for all of you,

that makes all things new.

Encounter the Man who died to rise to life,

all to know you.

THANK YOU NOTE

I hardly know where to begin. I am overwhelmed with gratitude.

To Allie Elmore, you are and have been my greatest champion though this whole process. I would not be the writer, the woman, and the friend I am today without your confidence and belief in me. Thank you for holding continual space for me and giving me courage in moments of insecurity and vulnerability. I love you and my gratitude for your friendship is immense. Cue, "That's What Friends Are For" by Dionne Warwick.

To my mom and dad, thank you for never failing to provide for and champion me in my dreams. My eyes swell with tears when I think of all you have ever done for me. Because of your consistent belief and provision, I know there is nothing that is unattainable. I know anything is possible. It has given me the ability to dream unlike most, and I will never not be thankful for you both. I love you so immensely.

To my grandmother, my grandpa, and my entire family—you mean the world to me. I carry you, dearest, in my heart always.

Because of you, I can beat anybody in a board game—and *without* cheating, Uncle Ricky.

Grammy, thank you for all the hours of growing up playing Scrabble together. My immense love for words and their ways was cultivated by all the years we sat together in your living room—a bowl of popcorn beside us—dictionary open, discovering just how much mere letters could form meaning. You're one of my favorites of all time, I love you.

To all of my dear friends and community that have walked with me for years, consistently seeing and believing in me—I could not have done this with without you. I see you. Thank you. I love you.

To Carrie Lloyd and Hannah Babarskis, thank you for your leadership and covering in this process. I could not be more grateful for and honored by the caliber of women I have fighting for me in my corner.

To Gable Price, my brother, thank you for always believing in my writing. You are a hero to me. Never forget when I beat you in NBA 2K.

To Chloe Beth Kerr, excuse me, woman, you are one phenomenal and brilliant creative genius. Thank you beyond and beyond for all you have poured into the design and craft of this book. I felt so fought for by you in how well you stewarded and brought to life my vision for *Iridescence* with such care and intentionality. It has been the utmost and greatest honor to do this with you. You are so filled with the Spirit of God and this is, and would not have been, without you—massive cheers to you, my girl!

To Tim Boddenberg, Printopya, and my faithful editor, Chelsea Slade. Thank you so much for your help, care, and investment in bringing this fully to life. It has been an honor to do this with you.

To any and all readers, thank you for taking the time to read my heart spilled onto a page. Writing poetry is an extremely vulnerable, important, and wonderful thing. Your choice to read these words matters to me and I pray you can relate and know, inside all of your experience, that there is no alienation or shame. I pray you can find courage to spill your heart out too. It's worthy. I honor you.

Forever grateful,

Micaela

NOTES & ACKNOWLEDGMENTS

"Illuminating Love" was a prayer inspired and awakened by Strahan Coleman.

In "At the Periphery," the configuration "To understand, to truly listen, you must reach out of your condition" is a phrase rearranged and borrowed from Mary Oliver's poem "Leaves and Blossoms Along the Way" that led to inspiration for this poem.

"Beauty can both shout and whisper" was a line that was inspired by Mary Oliver in the poem "Felicity," as well as the majesty of the mountains in front of me.

"The Triteness of Being" carries a phrase that was inspired by Mary Oliver's "Felicity":

 "The hardest questions of life are the most interesting."

In "The Cost," the line "beware the barrenness of business" is a quote from the brilliant and ever beautiful Amy Alexander.

In "If Just for a Moment," yes, I'll answer your question here—no, it was not intended to reference this nor was I thinking of it in that moment, but yes, I love the movie *Perks of Being a Wallflower*. Soft smile.

"No Flaw or Weakness" respectively lifts, borrows snippets, and alters small stanzas from Mark Nepo's poem "Breaking Surface" held within his book *The Way Under the Way*.

"Let the Veil Be Torn" is highly inspired from Mark Nepo's book *The Way Under the Way*.

In "This Body," the line "the pleasures of heaven you carry, the pain of hell you've felt..." is reconfigured and refers to a line from Walt Whitman's "Song of Myself."

"Whispering Alabaster" is incredibly inspired and entirely refigured from one of my favorite and most emotionally moving poems, Ocean Vuong's *On Earth We're Briefly Gorgeous*. This poem shares structure, ideas, and a phrase, "thirst is what holds me here."

"Turn Me into a Lily" was enlightened, with small lines reconstructed, from Weyes Blood's incredibly well-written song "Oh God, Turn Me into a Flower."

The poem "Space for You" was brought about from Mark Nepo's quote "I would do anything for you, would you be yourself?" Also, the friend whose repentance moved me was Laila Elk.

Laila, your heart is pure, humble, moving, and beautiful. I want to be as humble and pure as I saw you in that moment. I love you, my friend.

"Grief Can Be Bright" is completely influenced by a hero, Melissa Helser, from one of her teachings that left me a mess—in tears: "Grief is never to be void of the spirit of the illumination of God; it is independency that is at war with discerning light."

Small phrases in "Kindred" and "Passenger Seat", specifically including the line "we're nearly Earth already", was borrowed from a complete stranger who is one of my favorite poets and is an unashamed muse, @cowpokekennedy *(If you ever cross this randomly, please publish your own book)*

"Ache" was affected by a vivid memory of watching a dear friend simply bowl at a bowling alley and being overcome with love for them. It was then spilled out from the awe-striking poem "Let It Enfold You" by Charles Bukowski.

ABOUT THE AUTHOR

Micaela Fox is an artist, poet, entrepreneur, mystic, friend, and lover. She is originally from where the wind sweeps down the plains and where the waving wheat sure smells sweet—good ol' Mustang, Oklahoma. The wheat fields formed her; it was there she wrote one of her first poems at the age of eight. Rich in the southern vocabulary of fixin' and y'all, this small-town girl is now currently based in Dallas, Texas.

She is filled with a passion to unveil beauty and mystical truths to the world—binding together all that is holy and held within our being, whether through words or her photography. An adventurer, she has now traveled all over the world drawing out the marrow of this life through writing, captivated with an unrelenting love for the depths of Jesus, humanity, and intimacy.

With a heart for reformation and reconciliation, she believes poetry holds the invitation for others to be reconnected and awakened to the wild, vast expanse of their own hearts.

She lives for this: to *awaken* others to truly see and know the vastness of the love and beauty that is always present, all around and within. Love and beauty that carry the uncontainable and ever-glorious reality of oneness that restores all things.